THE 7 STAGES
OF
CREATIVITY

DEVELOPING YOUR CREATIVE SELF

JAMES A. WHITTAKER

ACKNOWLEDGEMENTS

Thanks to the employees of Microsoft Corporation and the many conference attendees who sat through countless hours of this course. Without your enthusiasm for the subject matter and your thoughtful feedback, the material in this book would not have matured to the point it has.

Special thanks goes to my brain scientist cohorts: Bailey Whittaker, my daughter and teacher who delights in the tiniest details of brain function. I may have had a hand in making your brain, but it is you who have wielded it to such perfection. Leland Holmquest, my friend and colleague who dug further into the neuroscience literature than I had and helped rework some of my ideas and prove others. Both of you changed the direction of this book and taught its author a thing or two.

Thanks also to Tony Angell and Angela LaRocca who read and commented on early versions of this manuscript and saw my creative processes first-hand in the learning and seeking phases through to the living final product. Thank you for your friendship and candor.

Finally, to my readers: I hope you enjoy this book and even more that it wakes up your inner creative genius. There is a world out there just waiting for your imprint. If this book helps you discover what lies inside your creative mind, then this will have all been worth the effort. Should you indeed discover that this book kick-starts your creativity journey, then visit the resources pages for this book at:

www.docjamesw.com/the-7-stages-of-creativity/

where slides, videos and links to additional material are kept and updated.

Enjoy!

The 7 Stages of Creativity

James A. Whittaker

Feeling uncreative? Lacking ideas about life, career and what to do this weekend?

You are not alone. It's not your fault. And - this is the best part - it's fixable. But first, let's discuss why you are here and feeling the way you feel.

You, like nearly every human on this planet, were born with an inquisitive, active mind that took you from knowing nothing in your infancy to where you are today. Your natural instinct for investigation and discovery powered you through your formative years as you consumed the world around you like a fearless little champion. You created your own games. You imagined your own entertainment. You envisioned your own future.

Then, somewhere along the way, life altered that natural course. It likely began in your early school years when you were woken before dawn and drug off to school to be bored to tears all day listening to unaccomplished people teach you things you didn't need to know and would never use in actual life.

The fact that we expend so much effort to convince young people that learning is a boring chore is at the root of our collective creativity problem. It's much of the reason that we ask questions we can't answer and live a life lacking purpose and conviction. But society's insistence on clogging our minds with waste-information will have to remain a mystery. That is not the problem we're going to solve in this book. Nor are we going to question the preteen social pressure to put aside individuality and embrace conformity or even the more grownup version of that process in which our employers expect us to put their priorities above our own.

The truth is that our creativity has many adversaries that aren't going anywhere any time soon. We can't fix the world, but we can cut away much of the scar tissue our schools and social institutions have caused so that we can once again flex the natural creativity that is our birthright. We may not be able to change the world, but we can change *you* and enable you to recapture that sense of awe and wonder that is a life spent in pursuit of instinctive learning and unbridled creativity. So read on and prepare for more ideas, a better life and, if you wish it, some serious career acceleration. For creativity is the conduit to an active mind and prosperous life.[1] You either have creativity or you want it back and either way this book will help you wield it like the creative little champion you really are.

Entering the creative class

Let's face it, we look up to the creative class. We wonder at both the ideas they generate and the lives they lead. Can you imagine spending your time contemplating the intricacies of life and mind and managing to live well as a result?

Creativity won't find you. You must find creativity.

Creative people do this. They transcend ordinary lives and ordinary careers. They don't experience the world around them so much as they bend it to their will, sometimes subtly and sometimes in ways that impact all mankind. Whatever your aspirations are for your own life and career, creativity will help you become the controller of your life rather than the victim of it. People who

---

[1] Neuroscientific research has often connected creativity with prosperity and well-being. At the end of this book, a list of references for further reading are provided that support this claim and provide details about the studies that demonstrate it. From Hirt, Devers, & McCrea (2008) showing that creativity helps sustain and promote feelings of happiness and purpose to Griskevicius, Cialdini, & Kenrick (2006) who connected creativity with our attractiveness to potential mates and Sligte, De Dreu, & Nijstad (2011) finding that creativity enables us to gain social and career power to, finally, Amabile (1996) who connected creativity and successful entrepreneurship. Regaining our creative mojo is a key ingredient to a good life and this book is going to show you how to do it.

ignore their own creativity will lead the life that others choose for them. Think about it: how much of your day is determined by your own will and desires and how much is dictated by the needs of your employer? You either become part of the creative class or risk living your life in varying forms of servitude to it.

To master the creative forces of your mind, you have to understand something about creativity: no one gets it for free. As much as we look up to creatives, we must stop thinking they are special, that somehow they were born creative and possess some innate talent that is off limits to the rest of us. It is this very idea of assuming that *some people have something that we do not* that is holding us back and keeping us from reaching our own creative potential.[2]

Take creatives like Thomas Edison and Marie Curie as examples. Do you think that if it hadn't been for Edison that the world wouldn't have lightbulbs? Or that without Marie Curie, who discovered radioisotopes, that we'd lack inventions like the x-ray machine? Of course not! Just because Edison is credited with inventing

---

[2] Recent research on self-learning bears this out. Flora (2016) in *Psychology Today* concluded that it isn't intelligence levels or learning styles that impact how much we know but, instead, our own insecurities about our innate ability. In other words, we *can't* simply because we think we can't and this has a debilitating effect on our ability to move forward in our creative endeavors. This lack of belief crosses gender, race, ethnicity and even educational boundaries. We bear the primary responsibility for holding ourselves back.

4

lightbulbs doesn't mean that someone else, perhaps Nikola Tesla, wouldn't have done it. Truth is, if neither Edison nor Curie had ever been born, other creative minds would have seized their chance to create something very similar. We'd be driving cars whether Henry Ford's vision allowed them to be mass manufactured or someone else managed to do it.

Creativity isn't like Santa Claus who visits only the worthy little boys and girls, bestowing them with fabulous gifts, and leaving the rest of us with a lump of coal. If Elon Musk hadn't given us mass market electric cars, Henrik Fisker might have. If Bill Gates hadn't popularized the PC, we all might be happily using Macs and crowning Steve Jobs as the world's richest human. Indeed, there is an argument to be made that the world might be better off living through Tesla's, Fisker's or Jobs' vision rather than those who actually got the credit.

The bottom line is that none of these creative people are as unique or as special as we make them out to be. Indeed, Marie Curie's case points to creativity as a result of environment rather than biology as she was in an extended family brimming with Nobel Prize winners (she, herself, won two and the Curie family five). Now her family's propensity for invention implies inheritance, but I think it much more likely that she was brought up in an environment that nurtured and celebrated ideas rather than *we were all just born this way.* After all, what have Curie's progeny—or Edison's, Gates' or Jobs' for that matter—managed to invent? That's right, exactly nothing. Predestination seems highly unlikely. In general, the children of famous creatives fall more into the Paris Hilton ilk (famous for being famous) rather than continuing some creative dynasty. Genetics don't seem to be a necessary ingredient of a creative life.[3]

The fact that all of these creatives are replaceable should bring us inspiration. When no one is special, that means *everyone* is special and in this attitude lies the key to being creative: when you accept the idea that you don't have to be special to be creative, you have just qualified yourself for being one of the world's creatives.

That's right *you* get to decide whether you want to live a creative lifestyle. Because creativity doesn't choose its host. It won't tap you on the shoulder

---

[3] In fact, I'd argue that even if genetics play a role in creativity, a creative person must still have the desire to live up to their creative potential. Children of creatives like Steve Jobs or Bill Gates are raised with privilege and in comfort. Creativity, as a mechanism for establishing a better life, simply isn't necessary for them. There is something to be said for the sheer desire for a better life that brings out the work ethic that it takes to learn enough to enter the creative class. Research bears this idea out. Kandler *et al* (2016) found that while qualities such as intelligence, extroversion, etc, are heritable, they have only weak correlation with creativity. Much more correlation was found between environmental factors and measureable creativity. If genetics plays a role, it is only minor. This is good news: your ability to create an environment that significantly impacts your creativity is completely in your own hands.

and introduce itself. It won't become part of your thought processes unless you invite it in. Edison, Curie, Ford, Musk and Gates all did that. They embraced the lifestyle of a thinker until thinking became habitual. When that happened, the ideas flowed and they hacked not only their own existence for the better but managed to affect the way others around them experienced the world. This route is open to anyone willing to embrace the life of a creative whether your aspirations are to change the entire world or only your specific corner of it. Creativity is a game anyone can play. You just have to decide to play it.

Playing that game is exactly what this book teaches you to do. It shows you how to embrace the lifestyle of the creative mind so you can watch your own mind become more creative in the process. Where you take that creativity is completely up to you but know that seizing it requires no specialized education or skills. It only requires the willingness to lay aside the bad habits you gained in school and at work and rethink your own learning processes and nurture your creative biorhythms so that you can start living a more creative life.

If you are ready to embrace that life, a richer life of more and better ideas, your next step is easy... turn the page.

Stage 1: Learning

Before you can create, you must know. In order to know, you must learn.

The one thing all creatives have in common is knowledge. They all know stuff. Whether that stuff is about science, art, botany, technology, whatever... they know *something*. It is a rare ignoramus indeed who has a great idea or solves a hard problem. Something does not come from nothing.

Take Einstein as an example. He invented the mind-bending theory of relativity *after* he became knowledgeable in astrophysics. It was his knowledge of the subject that fed his creativity and it was the time he spent studying and learning astrophysics that led to the creative ah-ha moments he is so well known for and that never would have happened had he failed to learn. Creativity requires something to work with and the only way to feed it is to learn something.

So the first stage of creativity is learning. The question, at this point, isn't really what to learn (that actually comes in Stages 2 and 3 so stay tuned) but how to learn more quickly than you were taught in school. The faster you learn, the more you learn. The more you learn, the more you begin to discover where your passions and ambitions lie so learning as much as possible about as many subjects as possible will help you make better choices in later stages.

Once again, you have your school system to thank for teaching you bad learning habits. When kids are taught that learning is an impersonal act of poring over static text trying to memorize facts and figures while listening to boring lectures, the desire for knowledge suffers. Kids hate to be bored and when knowledge is something you gain simply to regurgitate it onto some exam form, it makes the idea of learning a purposeless chore rather than the delight that it should be. No wonder kids seek out the oblivion of social media and mindless distraction of video games, the alternative is dullsville.

In reality, learning is the process of experiencing the world, thinking deeply about it and then picking and choosing the parts of the world you really want to become more knowledgeable about.

Creatives learn. Make your list today.

So, make a list right now of the things you either need or want to learn. Pick things that seem interesting. Add some things that might help you get ahead. Sprinkle in a few that would make you famous. Don't be shy! This is a grown-up version of *what do you want to be when you grow up* except that now you are listing the things that you might learn well enough to really get your creative-mojo into overdrive.

Once you make your list, step back from it and enjoy some good news: learning any of these things is easier now than it has ever been. Schools are no longer the educational monopoly they once were. In fact, schools are pretty much the slowest way to learn anything. Was learning to write code on your list? Well, you could take a 12-week class at the local college or you could take a one-hour online tutorial (to see if you even like it) followed by a 6-lesson course to really learn it well. See you just compacted 12 weeks of learning into a long weekend. That's what I call productive learning!

Was learning to play guitar on your list? You could ask your friend Jack who knows how to play "happy birthday to you" or you could go to YouTube and find one of the hundreds of experts who will pick through any song you want note by note, chord by chord with pause and rewind buttons in easy reach ensuring you don't miss a single detail. All of this without even leaving the comfort of your living room. [4] Educational convenience at its very finest.

Access to experts

Which brings me to my first point about learning: access to experts is the best way to learn. You see no matter what you put on your list just now, someone out there somewhere has already learned it. They've puzzled through the details and subtleties long before you even became interested in the topic. They've already had their "ah-ha" moments and made their intellectual discoveries. All their effort will save you time because you can assimilate their insights and make your own on top of theirs. And with experts no more than an

---

[4] Ok, so this is a first-world answer. I get that. But technology is also the third-world's best hope at a level playing field. It is much easier to get the Internet into the third world than it is to transplant brick-and-mortar schools and flesh-and-blood teachers. Technology has or will have an impact on how fast the entire world can learn. It's only a first-world answer for now.

internet connection away, learning has gotten a whole lot more convenient.

When you learn from experts, you are standing on the shoulders of giants. So the first question you should ask yourself when you put any item from your learning list is: where are the experts? Find them and you've just accelerated your way through Stage 1.

For example, as a college senior I had to learn current events for a seminar class I needed in order to graduate.[5] Where all the other students were stuck learning by reading newspapers and watching television news (this was a decade before the internet would become our de-facto news source), I had access to my father and brother who were both voracious news junkies. Listening to them argue the subtleties of the news and newsmakers of the day was far more efficient than absorbing them myself because they knew the politicians and personalities involved. They understood how certain events were connected historically. They had already absorbed the news and created educated conclusions about how certain stories might unfold.

With their knowledge as a guide, I smoked the class, achieving a level of knowledge about the world that no other student could match because

---

[5] The full story is told in *Career Stories* available on the Amazon Kindle store at:
http://www.amazon.com/gp/product/B017JDMIC8.

they were all learning in isolation. My access to experts with diverse and opposing views allowed me to ask questions and get deeper explanations. I often exceeded even the knowledge of the professor himself during that class and he deferred to my opinion quite often. Since then, the first thing I do when attempting to learn any new subject is to seek out the experts.

Which brings me back to my list reproduced above. When I decided to learn public speaking skills I sought out actual oratory experts. Instead of reading books and studying speaking skills and body language in the abstract. I began watching videos of speeches on YouTube and attended presentation classes offered by my employer. I even went to a session of Toastmasters. Indeed, it was Toastmasters that convinced me that not everyone who claims to be an expert, or even sounds like one, is actually an expert. You need to be picky when you select an expert to learn from. Take the time to really spec out the field of potential mentors and develop as diverse a list of experts as possible. Don't just assume that because they teach a class, they are any good at it. Anyone can become a teacher. Anyone can film a how-to video. Be picky!

Frankly, the quality of the people teaching public speaking at Toastmasters was so low I actually began nodding off in the first meeting I attended. Beware false experts. You cannot trust the contents of your mind with anything less than a true expert. Anyone can promise expertise but if you want to reach the level of expert (which you *do*, more on that in later chapters), then you need someone who can actually deliver. I walked out of that meeting and never looked back. Learning from someone who can't keep me awake isn't going to be good enough. Mentors set the bar and if you learn from someone who is *pretty good* at something then you aren't likely to exceed that bar. I had the same reaction to the so-called experts my employer hired. It struck me that I had found the reason why so many of our presentations were so damnably dull: we learned our trade from people who weren't very good at it.

Instead, I began focusing on speeches and speakers I found online. TED talks like those from Amanda Palmer and Al Gore (yes, Al Gore!) taught me how to manage an audience. Lectures from Carl Sagan and Neil De Grasse Tyson drew me in to the point that I forgot I was studying. That's exactly how good I wanted to get! Comedians like Mitch Hedberg, Demetri Martin, Ron White, Jim Jeffries, Donald Glover and Wanda Sykes taught me how to use humor and organize a good storyline. Political speeches from Winston Churchill (We Shall Never Surrender) and Martin Luther King (I Have a Dream) taught me how to evoke an emotional response in my audience.

I had found my mentors and began to understand why they were so effective for me. As a field, they were diverse in background, race, gender and age.[6] As individuals each had something specific I could identify with. I didn't learn my entire stage presence from any one of them. Instead, I learned part of my stage presence from each of them. From Palmer came my facial expressions. From Sagan my hand gestures. From Martin my props. From White my voice cadence. From King my flow and delivery. I became a mashup of every expert that managed to resonate with me. So even as I was mimicking them I was creating my own unique style.

The power of mimicry

The idea of mimicking experts is powerful. Mimicry is not only the highest form of flattery to those you mimic, but it is also a great learning tool for you. Keep in mind that they are *experts* which means your ability to improve upon what they know and how they act is limited. The things they say and the mannerisms they exhibit are those of *experts*. Until you also reach that status (which will begin in Stage 4 and culminate in Stage 5), be willing to copy the way they explain things and the

---

[6] Diversity plays more of a role in your learning than you might give it credit for. Learning from only a single source will limit your world view. Try to seek out experts of various ethnicities, genders, races and lifestyles to get as complete a picture as you can of the subject you are trying to learn. An open mind is an educated mind.

15

techniques they use to do so. Mimicking is an important part of the learning process.[7]

In college I used mimicry to deliver points in my current events course exactly as either my father or brother would make them. Today when I deliver speeches, I still mimic experts. I open just the way Amanda Palmer opens. When I handle props, I do so in a manner very similar to that of Carl Sagan. I think this is a version of *fake it before you make it* where you adopt an expert's panache until, over time, you end up making it your own. Like a basketball player copying the technique of Michael Jordan - if you are going to mimic someone, you could do far worse than mimicking the style of someone who is very, very good at what they do - you eventually learn to put your own twist on the technique and creating a one-of-a-kind *you*.

Reciprocal mentor relationships

It is sometimes the case, in fact a very happy case, when the mentor you attract is physically present. My PhD advisor in college was an in-person relationship and even though he had many PhD students, he spent far more time with me because we had what I call a reciprocal relationship. I was getting advice and knowledge from him and he was getting the chance to apply his knowledge in my study area of software reliability. He taught me

---

[7] Which is why most bands start out as cover bands singing the songs that better musicians created. Part of learning in any field means copying first, you know: fake it before you make it.

the math that made up my dissertation research and, in turn, I taught him the field of software reliability that opened up new publication opportunities for him. It was give and take. Where the rest of his students took far more than they gave back, our relationship was more balanced. So guess who he gave more attention to? Guess who he took more interest in helping? That's right me, the one who gave back.

Take your mentors seriously. If you buy the premise that access to experts is the best way to learn (and it is) then once you rope an expert, make sure they are incented to stay. Every meeting I had with my PhD advisor I came prepared and took his time seriously. I made sure that we had an ongoing project that progressed from meeting to meeting, in our case it was a joint paper we planned to submit for publication. Figure out a way to ensure that the experts you are learning from are getting enough from the interaction that they will see it as valuable and put more time and effort into teaching you.

I taught this concept to my son when he was first learning to play guitar. After going through a couple mentors who, while admittedly better than my son, didn't set a very high bar, we decided to go after bigger fish. We haunted live music venues chatting with various guitar players to determine their tolerance to teaching a teenager the ins and outs of the instrument. It only took a couple weeks to find a few suitable candidates. This is the first lesson in mentor-hunting. It works only if you try.

Like anything of quality in your life, you don't get good mentors for free.

At this point it was up to him us to provide the incentive for them to be the best possible teacher to accelerate his learning. We spent time getting to know them and their own needs and sure enough we found an opening. One of the guitar players willing to teach him had just lost his band's jam space. When we offered our home as a place to practice we became a perfect match, quid pro quo. My son now had an instructor actually incented to teach him. Access to expert? Check! An expert incented to teach? Check! No money changed hands but a lot of learning took place.

Indeed, my son later upped the ante when he learned that his new instructor had a dream to play Led Zeppelin's *Going to California* but lacked a mandolin player to accompany him. My son used the money he was saving on lessons and bought a mandolin to make that dream come true. He progressed from novice to expert in record time. To this day people are shocked when they see his skill and find out he's only been playing for a short while.

My son (left) playing a gig with his mentor Billy Landers.

Learning takes work. If you go it alone it takes even more work and you miss out on the insights and expertise of others. Intensive study might eventually work for you, but it is the slow way to obtain knowledge or acquire a new skill. So don't be afraid to reach out to experts and, to the extent that you can become valuable to them, they will speed up the learning process and transfer their own insights and experience to you.

The last point about mentors is that you can't expect too much of them. It is unlikely that you'll find a single mentor for every subject you ever want to learn. My son's guitar playing is a case in point. His first mentor played electric guitar in a cover band but my son aspired to being a singer-songwriter which meant finding an original artist and acoustic instrument expert. Enter mentor number two, an expert on musical theory and composition. Mentor number three was a gearhead who knew sound, pedals and special effects better than either mentor one or two. Mentor four was a musician who played by ear and taught him the subtleties of tone and exactly how to hold the fret board and strike the strings. Mentor five: vocals; six: piano. You get the picture. For everything you need to learn, find the best possible expert.

One subject generally equates to multiple mentors and rarely does a single mentor match multiple subjects. One person won't teach you to code and to fix motorcycles. Such a person is unlikely to be expert in both and good enough, well, isn't good enough! The quality of the expert matters and few people are going to be expert at everything you have on your list of things to learn.

When it comes to mentors, choose wisely. Ask yourself what you want to learn and who is best to help teach it to you. Give that a long ponder and then move on to Stage 2.

Learning Stage Presence - My Creative Journey Begins

In each chapter I am going to discuss my personal journey learning how to be a creative, successful public speaker. This first installment takes me from knowing nothing except how to talk to having a firm grasp on the body of knowledge I needed to acquire to become an expert.

My search for a real life stage presence coach came up empty. I just couldn't find a person I had physical access to that I thought would make an outstanding mentor. Remember my point about mentors setting the bar? Well I rejected several professional speaking coaches because they simply weren't right for me. They were professional and polished and way too corporate for my taste. I didn't want to be that kind of speaker. I wanted to be interesting and invoke passion in my audience. Step one is to eliminate the mentors that won't get you where you need to be. You don't have that kind of time to waste! The bar they set was too low for the type of presenter I wanted to become.

But one step down from mentor is *role model* and, thankfully, these are plentiful both online and at Microsoft where weekly speaker series and endless PowerPoint presentations helped me judge and reject dozens of speakers and develop my own *do* and *don't* lists. Often it was the negative examples (boy are there a lot of really bad speakers out there) that helped me learn. I began to call them "anti-mentors," i.e., people who were teaching me what *not* to do. Learning what not to do is still learning and as counterintuitive as it seems, learning what *not* to do is often as good a lesson as learning what to do. It serves to narrow the field of subject matter you have to master and, in a weird way, learning what not to do helps define what you actually end up doing.

During the learning phase it is important to be voracious. You are in learning mode, a receiver and cataloger of information. Since you never know what is going to be important, try to sample everything your subject has to offer. Treat the things you want to learn like a buffet, a little bit of this and a little more of that. Experiment! Make mistakes! Give up on some and take others for a longer test drive.

To learn stage presence, I watched a lot of TED talks and videos of comedians, always with a notebook so I could jot down what I liked and didn't like. I took note of where I laughed and where I lost interest. I hit rewind a lot.

In order to make a habit of my new learning regimen, I scheduled time at work and at home to watch a presentation at least twice a day. For presenters I liked, I watched everything they had to offer. I followed them on social media and discovered who they followed so I could also experience the people who influenced them. My net widened and I discovered a world of professional speaker circuits and training opportunities from places like Udacity, Udemy and The Great Courses that I did not know about before. Public speaking, it turns out, is big business and as I sought out the proper mentor I began to become pretty familiar with this business.

I experimented with the techniques I was cataloging by giving as many talks as I possibly could, both as part of my job and by creating speeches of my own and advertising them within Microsoft. This is where I learned 'fake it before you make it' by mimicking the delivery of the presenters I admired and aspired to be like. Microsoft conference rooms acted as a testing ground for the things I was learning and when I bombed I discarded the techniques I was using. When I garnered laughs or provoked admiration, I doubled down. When the audience members wanted selfies[8] with me after a particularly good presentation I watched the recording over and over to understand how my technique was beginning to really pay off.

Then I took my show on the road to conferences presenting Microsoft's developer story and later its advertising story. You can search my name on YouTube[9] and find a ton of activity during this time. Check the dates of my talks and see how I progressed over time. Once I learned what to do I went on to the next step, which is exactly where we are going right now. Time for Stage 2.

---

[8] Taking a selfie with a celebrity is the new autograph. When someone asks for a selfie, they liked what you did. It was a clear signal to me that my technique was beginning to work. Watch for such signals and gather whatever data you can that indicates you are growing in your craft.

[9] Links to my videos on YouTube, Channel 9, LiveArena and docs.com can be found on my website at www.docjamesw.com.

Stage 1 Cheat Sheet and Marching Orders:

- Learn something. You will never become creative by knowing nothing.

- Learn a lot of things because you don't know what is going to stick. Learn some career things, fun things, useful things and interesting things. Make a list and rock it.

- Learn from experts. Someone else has already learned what you want to know, use them as your guide, mimic them, absorb their knowledge to accelerate your own.

- Figure out how to keep your mentors involved in your journey. The more incented they are to teach, the more you will learn.

- One mentor per subject. No one is an expert on everything.

Stage 2: Thinking

When learning coalesces around a topic of extreme interest, the magic begins. As fast as you learned in Stage 1, now it's time to slow down and "catch yourself thinking."

You can learn all you want but if you don't spend a lot of time thinking about a subject, whatever you manage to learn will eventually fade to black. This is why you remember so little of what you learned in school. Despite intensive study, you never had reason to dwell lovingly on conjugating foreign verbs, computing a tangent or remembering the order the states joined the union. Unless your brain cooperates by dwelling on a subject, you have little chance of cementing any knowledge you gain from intensive study. Whatever you manage to learn is going to atrophy if your mind fails to ever return to it.

Of course, you could keep forcing your brain to turn back to a subject, but why would you? Why spend time learning something your brain is clearly rejecting? The chances that you will be a creative genius in a subject your mind is actively telling you to abandon is *very* small. Listen to your brain, unless it is returning to a subject out of sheer fascination, the chances of carrying that subject into your creative future is isn't very likely.

Mindfulness

The idea here is to "catch yourself thinking" and it is just about as hard as it sounds. In essence you have to actively think about what you are actively thinking about! It means being mindful of where your mind is wandering on its own and then notice when it returns to the same topic over and over again. That's the only way to really understand the subjects your mind is truly interested in (and can get creative about).

As I look at my list from the last chapter, several things were learned and rejected. I became a soccer referee but it lost its appeal after a couple of seasons. I learned some notes on the harmonica but had to force myself to practice and never (not once) found my mind wandering on its own in the direction of my harmonica. My mind was simply unwilling to go there on its own and this is a sign that any real mastery I obtained over these subjects would require a lot of work. I'd have to keep forcing myself to return to that same work again and again because my brain simply wasn't cooperating. You remember this feeling about a bunch of things you had to learn that your mind wasn't really interested in. It's called homework.

The subjects that you have the most chance of being creative with are the subjects that you think about without having to be reminded or forced. You think Michael Jordan's mom had to remind him to practice basketball? Of course not, she probably had to remind him to *stop* practicing. You think Jimi Hendrix's parents had to set a schedule for guitar practice? Not a chance. That is how he got so good and rarely does anyone get to that level of expertise against their will.[10]

You see when you find your mind drifting to a subject on its own, this is a very strong sign that it is a subject you can ultimately master. Thinking, especially when it is voluntary and enjoyable, takes learning to the next level.

So take a good look at your list from the last chapter and consciously remember how often your thoughts stray to that subject over the course of a day or a week. My mind was very active around the subject of stage presence. I could see myself on stage delivering powerful lines and keeping my audience's attention. I found myself looking forward to my next talk and lamenting weeks where I didn't have a presentation to give. By far, public speaking was at the top of my learning list. Of all activities I could pursue, I knew public speaking was one I was likely to get good at and make creative contributions to. Writing is

---

[10] Sarah Chang (https://en.wikipedia.org/wiki/Sarah_Chang) is a wonderful example of this. She learned one finger piano playing at an early age and then begged her mom for more time on the piano every day. Her mind chose for her and by following her mind's passion she became a violin virtuoso in a short period of time and is known as one of the greatest players of all time.

second. My mind strays to it quite often (as you might guess sitting there reading my words!) and I rarely have to schedule time to force myself to write. Put a laptop in my hands, and I am very likely to use my word processor before my email client or social app.

Nothing else even came close which explains why I'll never referee a professional soccer match or play harmonica like Neil Young. I'll never naturally think about either of these things enough to become an expert.

Find your passion

But what happens if all the learning in the world takes you no closer to a subject that interests you so much that your thoughts wander to it unbidden? Well, in that case you need to widen your net. Take a long hard look at the world. There is enough diversity in it that you'd be a rare human indeed who couldn't find *anything* worth lingering over. If you are having a hard time finding something to occupy your mind, then you need to get out more and sample the sheer wonder of life. That's right, put that selfie stick down. Back away from your Facebook shrine. It's time to take a long look at the world around you and rediscover its mysteries. Don't be afraid to broaden your horizons and take a bigger-picture approach to life.

Here are some ideas to get you started. Start going to museums and reading travel sites. Look at the worlds of technology, fashion, sports, ecology, gaming, politics, writing, entertainment, travel, science, art, construction, law, dance, education, publishing, entrepreneurship, marketing, design, nature... Someone should write a book about the diversity of activity available to humanity, but until they do you'll have to do your own home-work using the Internet, television, magazines and the library if you want to go old school. Open your mind, open your heart and clear your schedule - you have some hunting to do. Remember, your creative lifestyle is at stake so take this seriously and never stop looking until you've found that subject that ranks pretty close to food and sex as enjoyable ways to spend your free time. And when you do, rejoice! Creativity is in your future.

Bill Gates found his interests in computers. For Henry Ford it was the car. For Marissa Mayer it was information retrieval. Elon Musk started with digital payments, moved to electric cars, then solar power and finally colonizing Mars. He may yet have a few more chapters to write. Every creative who has made a name for him/herself has started with the subject that they just couldn't stop thinking about.

What's yours? Can you develop the ability to catch yourself thinking? Start practicing because the act of thinking is often involuntary as your mind strays to places of interest. Once you identify the subjects your mind naturally gravitates to, you've mastered Stage 2. Congratulations, you've become a thinker.

Thinking led to a passion and passion led to doing.
Can mastery be far behind?

Here's the thing about thinking: it activates the mind and allows it to really dig into a subject. When you start mulling a problem over the problem grows familiar. This familiarity accelerates learning and the more you learn about a subject the more interesting that subject becomes. When things are interesting they become enjoyable. When they are enjoyable, you keep doing them which means even deeper learning. It's a virtuous cycle that will cause you to think more about a subject just because it is enjoyable to do so, which only causes you to learn that much more and invoke even more thinking and even more joy.

This perfect storm of self-perpetuation is called *passion*. Picture Jimi Hendrix digging so hard into his chord progressions he forgets the audience is even there. That's passion. Remember Michael Jordan streaking down the court with his tongue wagging in sheer delight. That's passion. It's what happens when you find *that thing* that interests you and really allow it to take over your thought process. Active thinking turns into passion. And passion turns into mastery, but mastery is a subject for Stage 5… you still have some ways to go before you get that far, but once passion strikes you can rest assured you *will* get there. Your passion will see to that.

Passionate people can't help but to pour a large amount of energy into their work. Why wouldn't they? They are doing something intensely interesting that provokes great joy. Of course they are going to want to spend as much time on it as possible. And when their mind has a moment to go idle, it will drift into thinking about their passion.

Once passion strikes, you're pretty much finished with this phase. Trust your instincts and just allow that passion to guide you. Over time it will lead you to your creative center and along the way you are going to be doing really interesting work that you glean a great deal of enjoyment from. Who wouldn't want that?

Passion needs a guide

The passions of Gates, Ford, Mayer, Jordan, Hendrix... powered their learning and increased their knowledge over that of their peers. But passion also needs a guide. Pure passion alone can take a person in many unproductive directions and overwhelm warnings meant to protect you from bad investments and business decisions. It is important to continuously question your growing passions lest they take over your more cautious reasoning processes.

This is particularly important if you need your passion to provide a living.[11] You should question the validity of your passions as to whether they will be worthwhile and productive:

- Asking yourself if anyone else will care about your passion.

- Being realistic about how much value society will place on your passion regardless of how much you love it.

- Understanding how much longevity your passion will have. Thinking about its long term relevancy and your own ability to not get burned out because you are spending so much time on something that ultimately becomes a fad.

---

[11] When passion is applied to your day job, serious career acceleration can be the result. Imagine getting paid for doing something you fundamentally love to do? But merging passion and work isn't the point of this book. That subject is covered in *Career Superpowers* available at: https://www.amazon.com/dp/B00MEOV48C.

Let's say that the Dungeons and Dragons topic was the one topic I was most passionate about from my list from the last chapter. What then? Could I take it somewhere? Would writing and publishing adventure guides be enough for me? How would I monetize that work? How long could I continue it before it no longer consumed my waking mind?

Bill Gates' story is a cautionary tale of over-focus on a passion. His mindset was so fixed on desktop computers that he failed to see both the web and mobile coming. When laptops came out, he never saw them as mobile devices, just desktop computers that were more portable. Never did his fixed mind grasp the idea that as a mobile device it could transcend the PC because it could be carried along with you wherever you went. He was blind to any possibilities outside his beloved Windows and the web came along and blindsided him. Then the mobile device deluge from Apple (iPod, iPhone and iPad) nearly swept everything Microsoft stood for into the dustbin of history. As much power as his early passion bestowed on him, it morphed into a bad case of single-mindedness.

Once passion really sets in, you have to watch it closely lest it turn into its evil evolved state of obsession. Passionate people tend to focus on narrow aspects of their work and that can blind them to other areas that might lead to bigger and better things. In the next section, we'll deal with ways to begin probing your passion for direction, like asking questions similar to the following:

- What are all the parts involved in this thing you are passionate about?

- What all can you do with it beyond the obvious?

- How can you get other people involved in helping you with it?

- How can you take it to the next level?

- What questions do you have about it?

- Can you break it down into its constituent parts so you understand it in its totality?

These sorts of questions can help guide further thinking on a topic that you become passionate about. For example, as I contemplated stage presence and the techniques I can use to more fully engage my audience these types of questions remind me that it isn't just about my performance on stage, I need to widen my perspective to include things that have nothing to do with the stage itself. I need a good website so any fans I generate have a place to go to follow me. If I am going to monetize my work, I need to have discoverable books, videos and podcasts for sale.

Passion is a multi-headed beast and when thought turns to passion you must be vigilant. Passion will lead you into the world of the creative but whether that world ends up being worthwhile and productive might require some work on your part. You'll only find out by becoming a thinker.

Thinking About Stage Presence - My Creative Journey Continues

Digging into stagecraft created a desire within me to get really, really good. I found myself disgusted with the state of presentation skills by my peers at Microsoft and within the industry. I finally allowed myself to admit just how bored I was at conferences and in conference rooms. I entertained myself by silently mocking the presenter and mentally tallying every mistake I witnessed. It became one of my favorite games to "count the sins" of presenters. My interests in the presentation arts began to take hold.

I also began mental practice of my own by imagining myself on stage and delivering my message powerfully to a rapt audience to the point that they remember me and my message for years afterward (I am told this happens quite often now). If only I had a guitar in my hands, I would have been an imaginary rock star! This line of thinking led me to treating my presentations as a "set list" that musicians use to remember the order of their songs. I began structuring my talks in a similar way and it helped me remember all the points I wanted to make. Already my constant attention to my subject was beginning to pay dividends.

The time I spent intensely thinking about stagecraft helped me realize that every talk has 3 basic parts: a strong start, delivering my message and a compelling ending with takeaways. Breaking it up this way allowed me to begin thinking in more detail about the individual parts: *how* to start strong, *what* my message actually was and *how* to end a talk on a thoughtful note. Breaking my learning into parts allowed me to concentrate on each individual piece and increase my level of understanding of its specifics. I found that as my mastery of each part grew, my knowledge of the greater whole increased substantially.

Being really thoughtful about watching other experts (and anti-experts) and my own practice ensured that every time I went on stage, I was a little better than the last time. I could feel the approach of mastery and it was intoxicating.

Stage 2 Cheat Sheet and Marching Orders:

- Catch yourself thinking. When your mind drifts to a subject on its own, that is a strong indicator that you have found something of extreme interest.

- Double down on it. Learning a subject deeply is what it takes to become creative. Narrow your field of study to the thing your mind is wandering to on its own.

- Watch for passion to strike. Once it does, buckle up and enjoy the ride. You are on your way to becoming a self-powered learner.

- Remember, if you are relying on your creativity to earn a living make sure that your passion is aimed at something people actually care about.

Stage 3: Seeking

Once curiosity takes over, expertise can't be far behind.

As you are learning and thinking, I want you to keep an eye out for one of the most powerful investigative and educational devices in the known universe: curiosity. When curiosity surfaces, rejoice! Seriously, open that bottle of champagne you've been saving. Treat yourself to a fancy restaurant. Buy yourself a new outfit. You have just entered Stage 3 where serious creative momentum begins. Indeed, curiosity is so powerful that even mighty Einstein credited it - and not his intelligence or technical skill - for his ability to invent mind-bending concepts like the theory of relativity. Curiosity and creativity are clearly close siblings.

Curiosity is far more than simple interest in a subject. It is a *desire*... a *need* to know more. It is an insatiable drive to understand and to master.

 James Whittaker @whojamesw Feb 20
Every skill and piece of knowledge you possess has its roots in curiosity. Be curious about the world and the world will reveal its secrets.

As such, curiosity isn't intentional so much as it is

instinctive. You can't force yourself to be curious, however, you can tempt curiosity out by understanding that it surfaces after you've thought deeply about a subject. So in Stage 2 as you're pondering the nuances of a subject, keep a watchful eye out for curiosity. It will likely begin as you learn enough about a subject that its intricacies seem less mysterious and its subtleties clearer. It's almost as though your brain is proud of itself for learning enough to develop some understanding and it now wants to know more all on its own. This is a really good sign of approaching creativity because curiosity means you have a natural affinity to a subject and becoming a creative within you field of study is within your reach.

But let's not get ahead of ourselves. Once curiosity emerges, you still have to harness its power and learn to wield it toward mastery of the subject at hand. That's the process we're going to tackle in this chapter: what to do when curiosity emerges. The answer comes in two forms: asking questions and performing thought experiments.

Ask questions

Let's take up questions first. Understanding their power will help you wield your curiosity like a champ.

Curiosity naturally leads to questions. Remember asking 'why?' as a kid? You did this because you were curious and curious people ask questions.

Curiosity demands answers and once you've learned enough to start asking your own questions, there is only one thing to do: seek answers to those questions.

When you, and not some teacher or mentor, become the questioner you've entered the seeking stage of creativity. Questions are a sign that you've absorbed enough of a subject to begin seeking a deeper level of understanding. The fact that your curiosity has surfaced is a really good sign. It will make you *want* answers which means your learning is now self-propelled. You are working off your own need to know rather than chasing some external benefit or learning something because a teacher or manager wants you to. This *desire to know* is a powerful force. Celebrate it. All those questions will eventually lead to expertise, which is a key ingredient for creativity.

A question is a powerful learning motivator because a question demands an answer. It forces a very specific investigation, not for investigation's sake (that was the previous stage) but in order to find an answer. Asking 'what if' isn't just a question. It is a specific experiment that helps frame your tactics in looking for an answer. Asking the question 'why is this hard?' or 'what are the alternatives?' will guide you toward proposing possible answers and alternative means of investigation and thinking through potential outcomes. You see, questions force your mind to come up with answers. As long as the answer remains elusive, you know you are still seeking. Once the question is fully answered, it's time for the next stage.

When you seek answers to the questions that are now swirling in your head, you move toward even deeper understanding and begin to amass expertise. The right questions can guide you toward a creative answer. When Amazon asked the question 'what would it take to order diapers in 10 seconds?' they ended up creating the hugely successful Echo. When Niantic Labs asked the question 'how might one play Pokémon in the real world?' the result was Pokémon Go, a product that eclipsed even internet giant Twitter's traffic the first week it launched. It was the framing of the question that led to the innovative answer. Seek and sometimes you might find something really creative!

Questions are important. Ask them. Write them down. Let them be your guide as you investigate the subtleties of the subject you are learning.

Let's take Gates' goal of *a computer on every desk and in every home* as an example. This simple but sweepingly broad goal forces some serious questions to be asked, and that's one reason it was such a successful motivator. Questions like: what software would it take for consumers to find a computer useful enough to have one in their home? How would you go about getting developers to write that software? What mechanisms for getting useful software on those computers would be necessary? How do you manage to manufacture enough computers to make this a reality?

Can you see how such questions guided the way Microsoft executed its strategy? Products like Word, PowerPoint and Excel were the best answers to the usefulness query. Collaborating with hardware companies like IBM, HP and Dell ensured availability of hardware and the production of developer tools and libraries ensured there would be enough developers writing code to continuing making computers useful. Microsoft's goal made them ask questions and those questions led to answers that made the world want computers.

Likewise, Henry Ford's questions about mass production and pondering what it would take to get there, led him to the idea of the assembly line. He asked whether the assembly line could be made efficient enough so that the people working on the assembly line could actually afford to buy the cars they were making. These questions act as both the impetus to investigate and a guide to implementing the idea. In order for cars to be cheap enough for middle class buyers, he had to learn how to build a better assembly line to drive down price. The goal sparked the questions. The questions guided the investigation. The investigation provided the answers.

Answers, you see, follow directly from questions. You can't be a seeker without first having something to seek so start asking as many questions about your chosen subject as you can.

Sometimes it is the simplest questions that make the most impact. The first time I ever got to the seeking stage of creativity was when I was in graduate school studying software testing. I asked the simple question *Why is testing so hard?* The investigation[12] this question provoked lasted a couple of semesters and was one of the most intense learning periods of my life, turning up 4 fundamental answers. The resulting paper[13] describing those answers was one of the top 25 downloaded papers in the history of the most prestigious magazine in computer science, cementing my reputation as a top thinker in the field. My reputation and subsequent career acceleration came from the questions I was asking.

This is how questions help you focus. Instead of a sea of details that might confuse or overwhelm you, questions let you start with something simple and then guide you to the details in a consumable, manageable way. As I pondered *why is testing so hard*, I didn't have to think about *how* to actually perform testing or *what* technique might work better in a certain situation. I was focused on the

---

[12] This journey is documented more fully in my book *Career Superpowers*. Available in eBook form here:
https://www.amazon.com/dp/B00MEOV48C.
[13] Published in *IEEE Software*, Vol 17. No 1, January 2000. Available at:
http://ieeexplore.ieee.org/xpl/articleDetails.jsp?arnumber=81997 1.

single question of *why* and as I went through the process of testing in my head I quickly compiled of list of the things that made it hard. As I continued to reflect on them,[14] I whittled each down to exactly four things that caused the most work and were the most prone to error. My insights clearly resonated with a lot of people who tested software as the popularity of the paper was near viral.

So ask questions. Lots of questions! What are you curious about? Knowledge isn't going to find you. You must be the seeker and root it out and asking questions that help focus your investigation is a great way to accomplish this. Remember the Amazon Echo came from the simple question *how could a customer order diapers in less than 10 seconds?* Pokémon Go was the result of asking *how might someone play Pokémon in the real world?* You see, every creative solution begins by asking the right questions.

---

[14] Modern psychologists and neuroscientists have called this mental problem solving state *flow* to capture the flow of thoughts that come as a result of discovery and sequential understanding. A more colloquial term might be "in the zone" wherein your mental state is engaged and focused. Study of this concept was pioneered by Mihaly Csikszentmihalyi and recent studies such as that by McGuinness (2015) have more shed light on the phenomenon. The results follow the method I prescribe herein: begin by learning a subject, gain expertise and allow your creative processes to guide an intuitive flow of thoughts. Stay tuned, this flow will eventually lead to a slip-stream in later stages where ideas move from a gentle stream to an unstoppable river.

Thought experiments

Next, let's turn to a related concept called *thought experiments.* Thought experiments are mental exercises that help you answer your curiosity induced questions by designing experiments that you conduct inside your own head. Popularized by Albert Einstein's famously simple ways to answer deep questions[15] without messy mathematics and details to get in the way. Thought experiments are ways to guide your mind through a problem at a conceptual level instead of wallowing in confusing details. They are intentionally high level so as to investigate the big picture of a problem which will set the stage for figuring out the details later. It's a sneaky approach, but so very strategic.

This is important: thought experiments don't contain details. This makes them perfectly suited for developing your creativity because most really creative ideas are not detailed. Instead, they are high level concepts like Gates' *a computer on every desk and in every home* or Ford's assembly line. The concept sets the stage for the details, which makes it the most important part of the creativity equation.

---

[15] Einstein is credited with the idea of thought experiments but surely was inspired by ancient philosophers who used very similar processes many thousands of years ago. When a technique stands such a test of time, it pretty much has to be useful. Know that as you conduct your own thought experiments you are part of a historical chain of thinkers that goes back to Aristotle and Socrates. That's good company you are keeping!

Thought experiments have a huge advantage over prototyping in that they are extremely inexpensive (as they are mostly performed inside your own head) and the risk of failure is zero. If the experiment fails, you learn and move on to another experiment. The power to traverse complex models and connections in thought experiments cannot be overstated. The big picture can be developed and communicated in compelling ways before a single dollar is spent on a single detail.

For example, Einstein's argument that acceleration and gravity were one and the same would be hard to visualize mathematically but his thought experiment (described below) convinced even the most skeptical astrophysicist that he was right, prompting them to get to work on the details instead of arguing about the concept.

Einstein's Man-in-a-Box Thought Experiment

Imagine a box in outer space with a man inside it. In the absence of gravity, the man would float inside the box.

Now imagine that box suddenly lands on a planet. The man would be pulled to the floor of the box by gravity. Return him to space and he would begin floating again.

Alternatively, if a spaceship were to attach a cable to the box and accelerate, the man would also be

> pulled to the floor of the box as it moved. Stop accelerating and he would begin to float again.
>
> Gravity and acceleration have the exact same effect on the man in the box.

There are no rules concerning how to conduct a thought experiment. Most of them begin with a simple setup "suppose you have this situation" and then a description of the chain of events that flow from the setup. It's so simple, chances are you are already good at it. Give it a try and experiment with the subject you want to get creative with. Have fun exploring the places your own delightful and unique mind will take you.

When it came to my own knowledge quest concerning public speaking, I used questions and thought experiments in turn. I framed questions around other speakers' work to help lead me to the specific reasons they were so ineffective:

- At what point did I tune this presenter out? This helped me understand just how fast people get bored and led me to inject interesting anecdotes and techniques throughout a presentation and not just in one big dramatic climax.

- What did the presenter say that confused me? This helped me be alert for ways to ensure a simple, consistent message.

- What is the presenter's message and how could she/he have made that clear? Watching closely for the message helped me better frame my own central themes and takeaways.

- What are my takeaways from this presentation? Are the clear? If not, what is keeping them from being clear? The only way for a presentation to live on after the applause is for it to be memorable and applicable to the lives of the audiences. This question helped me focus on how to do that.

I took copious amounts of notes during this time based on questions like this. These questions helped me hone in on specific mistakes and learn from them rather than from some vague sense that the speaker was "just boring." The questions helped me get to the heart of the matter.[16]

I also framed more positive questions for my investigative work to help me generalize what I was learning:

- What makes a message really clear? Here my investigation went to language forms that were simple and memorable.

- What is the best way to deliver a really important detail? This question led me to techniques like metaphor and helped me

---

[16] Wilkinson (2015) calls this "driving for daylight" paying homage to the journey which starts with a question and ends with a course of action that may or may not lead to an actual answer. Sometimes, the journey itself yields insights and activity that has intrinsic value. It is the "driving" that is more important than the actual "daylight."

discover how to add thoughtful pauses into my oratory.

- What is the most impactful way to start and end a presentation? I understood that I had to draw the audience in right at the beginning or risk losing them. This question helped me hone in on two of the most critical parts of a presentation, the start and end.

- How can I get a standing ovation? Understanding that I needed to evoke an emotional response in the audience led me to investigate what it took to do that.[17]

Do you see how these specific questions help focus my pursuit of stage presence? With these questions as my guiding principles, I am not just watching TED talks and comedians; I am focusing on their message and understanding when that message is and isn't clear. That's good, actionable data. I can watch for times where speakers both land and fail to land a point. More good data. I can watch the beginnings of 20-30 presentations specifically for patterns around strong and weak starts. Then I can fast forward to the end and watch whether they stick the landing (or not). My learning is guided by the questions I ask. The better the questions, the faster the learning.

---

[17] Standing ovations now are a regular occurrence at my presentations. The largest was some 6000 people at Tech Ready in Seattle in July 2016. And it all started with a question.

Now it's your turn. Become a seeker of answers and move a little closer to an innovative, creative you.

Seeking Stage Presence - My Creative Journey Continues

I hit the seeking stage very early in my quest for good stage presence. My curiosity was sparked almost immediately as I began to experience the thrill of being on stage and presenting to larger and larger audiences. As the laughter got louder and my storytelling more vivid, possibilities began to open up for me. Just by putting myself out there and getting noticed, I was invited to speak at CES, Cannes Lions, Digital Life Design, SXSW and Summit@Sea. These are big, prestigious venues for me to ply my new trade. It was my seeking that started all this and my growing ambition further fueled my desire to keep pushing myself toward bigger and better venues.

I challenged myself to be the best speaker at every event I went to and the rare times I wasn't, my ambition demanded I learn from the process and get better. I got good enough that my public challenge to Microsoft competitors to go head-to-head in a storytelling contest went unanswered.

Seeking sharply increased my skill and put me on the path to mastery. It helped me establish important industry connections first in the software developer world, then advertising and marketing and finally in the entrepreneurial and creative realms. My process to observe, question, discover, practice and refine ensured that I improved and learned. As others were drawn to my increasing talent, my opportunities to observe, question, etc., grew and I just kept getting better.

Stage 3 Cheat Sheet and Marching Orders:

- Watch for curiosity to emerge. When it does you've left the thinking phase and entered the realm of self-powered investigation. Mastery of your subject is going to happen.

- Document your curiosity by asking questions. Frame questions that help you seek the answers you need to further your knowledge acquisition.

- Perform thought experiments that allow you to investigate different solutions and angles. Try to figure out 'what would happen if'...

- Remember, whether you find the answers or not, you are learning your subject inside and out and are driving toward becoming an expert.

Stage 4: Focusing

Specialization narrows your world and allows you to really nail something.

Now that you have navigated through the learning and thinking stages and spent time seeking out your natural curiosity, it's time to introduce the next stage: focusing on getting *really* good at something. The good news is that your wonder and curiosity have led you to a subject you find genuinely interesting and that interest is going to accelerate your learning even more. The better news is that at some point the knowledge you gain is going to turn into genuine expertise. When that happens you have, yet again, cause to celebrate. Expertise is the key to unleashing your creativity. So strive to become a subject matter expert.

Expertise means getting really good at something to the point that much of your knowledge ceases to require active thinking and seeps into the long-term corridors of your brain where habits and instincts reside. Facts and figures can be recalled without active thought. Problems can be solved quickly without much mulling and your use of your knowledge begins to become instinctual.

People satisfied with being merely good at something don't experience this transformation from knowledge to instinct. The Jack's/Jill's-of-all-trades/masters-of-none are just good enough to demonstrate competence but not expert enough to really stretch the boundaries of their knowledge. They will only tread the well-worn paths of a subject instead of expanding its boundaries.[18] While that is fine for some careers and a useful thing for society, it will rarely induce a creative burst. Being pretty good usually makes you useful to other people and not a commander of your own fate. Becoming expert at one thing, i.e., focusing, allows a subject to be mastered and within that mastery is where creativity is born.

what you say	how you say it	what you do
script	state – pause – clarify	body language
logical consistency	descriptive language	movement
plot progression	tone of voice	props
	pace and cadence	choreography
	repetition	
	reality v aspiration	
	metaphor	
	story	
	audience connection	

Lots of things to get right on stage but mastery requires focus.
Time to pick one and focus on it.

---

[18] Specifically, McGuinness (2015) concluded that the flow of the mind or "getting into the zone" was generally off limits to people who fail to develop a certain level of skill and expertise.

The science behind how expertise transforms your brain is really quite interesting. Once you get really, really good at something you don't have to actively think about it so much because all the facts, figures and information are stored firmly in your brain and wielding your knowledge becomes instinctual rather than requiring active thought. This leaves your brain with excess capacity which you can use for creative thinking. In other words, your instinctual mind and your conscious mind get to collaborate and that is where the magic happens. The conscious mind can stray to new creative places because the instinctual mind can do most of the heavy lifting on its own.

Remember learning to ride a bike? It took a lot of active thinking at the beginning. You really had to focus on it. The conscious, thinking part of your brain was working really hard to figure out all the stimuli you were experiencing as you struggled with anxiety and fear while simultaneous trying to balance and propel yourself forward. But once you got the hang of it, instinct began to kick in and I bet that no matter how little you ride now, you have never forgotten how to do it. In fact, you are probably so good at it your active mind is free to roam where it will while your instinctual mind takes care of the semantics of pedaling, steering and balancing.[19]

---

[19] Significant recent research using *functional magnetic resonance imaging* (fMRI) has resulted in deeper understanding of how our brains work, specifically during periods of creativity (Beaty,

This collaboration between the instinctual part of your mind and the active thinking part is where creativity roams. Viola! You get to use two parts of your brain at once! This magical partnership happens automatically which is exactly the reason that some ideas just seem to hit us out of nowhere. The proverbial idea-in-the-shower is actually a real phenomenon because your mind has been wandering the fertile fields of creative thinking while the instinctual mind has you on autopilot. Your mind can be hard at work without you even realizing it.

This is the genesis of your creative power: Your deep, instinctual knowledge of a subject stored in the long-term corridors of your mind can be mulled over using the active thinking part of your

---

Benedek, Silvia and Schacter, 2016). Heightened metabolic activity has been observed in the midline and posterior inferior parietal regions of the brain during periods of creativity. Researchers have concluded that the process of creativity is accomplished by dynamic interactions between the default and executive control networks (Beaty, et al, 2016). Previously, the default network was thought to be associated with generative processes (i.e., imagining a future state) fMRI has shown that coupling this area with the control network is what is required to achieve goal-directed cognitive processes (Beaty, et. al., 2016) like being creative. Thus, neuroscience validates the stages that I have shared thus far. In order to be creative, one must have knowledge, as required by cognitive processes and seek answers to gain a deeper understanding. Once the brain is able to make the linkage between the knowledge one has *and* the ability to explore possibilities and combinations with others variables stored in the mind, creativity is unleashed (Beaty, et al, 2016). The default network influences the generation of new ideas, while the control network constrains and directs the process towards specific goals. Isn't your brain simply wonderful?

brain. It is the beginning of you as an idea factory. And it doesn't even require active thought. Even the process of procrastination means that our subconscious mind is still actively connecting information and resolving our understanding of the nature of some new or complex subject. You see, just because you have disconnected from a subject and moved on to something else, does not mean your brain has. It is often working on your behalf pondering your problems and working toward a solution.

What a magnificent organ we all possess between our ears.

The prior seeking stage tells you what interests you. But interest alone may or may not be enough to take you where you want to be. So let's perform some checks on where your thinking and seeking have taken you to see if it is a place that will provide good career opportunity. If you find out it isn't, you may want to return to the seeking stage for a while to see if you can find a focus area that will provide good opportunity. This is perfectly fine and not to be treated as a step backward, but more of a refinement of focus. Getting your focus right is much more important than getting it fast.

However, if interest is more important to you than opportunity, by all means start focusing *now*. Creativity awaits and ultimately the area you choose to be creative in must matter to you, whether the rest of the world finds it interesting or not.

Let's start with a couple of questions you can ask about the interests you discovered while you were seeking:

Can you actually master your focus area?

In order to use the long term corridors of your mind you have to learn a subject to the point that it becomes instinct.[20] So choosing a specialty that you can only get pretty good at is not really helpful to your creativity. Being pretty good means not standing out because it is a level that is obtainable by a lot of other people. Being pretty good makes you part of the crowd and whatever creativity you manage is very likely to be of the ordinary sort. If you are ok with that, then proceed. Otherwise, you might want to revisit the seeking phase to see if you can find something more easily conquerable.

Is the subject you've decided to master small enough to fit completely inside your head? Can you visualize mastery or are there barriers that seem too high to climb? My first job required me to transition from a software developer to a software tester and I immediately grasped the subject of testing as *my thing*. Development always seemed too open-ended and I kept getting

---

[20] We keep running into the need to be an expert at something. This is no accident. Every creative individual is an expert at *something*. Being an expert just keeps paying dividends and we're not through yet. In later stages, you will see this idea pop up again. If you take away nothing else from this book it should be the idea that you need to get really, really good at what you do.

surprised by things I didn't know and that seemed arcane to me. I knew I would never be more than a good-enough developer. There was so much to learn I was constantly overwhelmed by some detail that I had never before considered. But with testing, I could fit that subject in my head with room to spare. It seemed so much more approachable and consumable to me.

A natural, comfortable fit with a subject is a really good sign. The further you have to reach, the more of your mind you'll need for learning and the less you have available for thinking and seeking and, ultimately, creating. So give your subject matter a test to see how good a fit it is:

- [Stage 1: learn] Do I have access to excellent mentors and other learning tools I need to completely master this subject?

- [Stage 2: think] As I think about the subject do I enjoy it? How fast does understanding come? How often am I stressed when new details emerge?

- [Stage 3: seek] Am I naturally curious about the subject. Does it enter my mind unbidden? Does thinking about it make me happy?

Testing was so perfect for me because I had secured long term and reciprocal relationships with expert teachers whose presence increased the probability of true mastery. Whenever I actively thought about the subject I learned something new and became excited about the prospects of a career doing it. When my natural curiosity was sparked, I knew I had a winner. This same progression happened later when I learned computer security and again when I focused on stagecraft.[21]

So ask yourself whether you and the subject you have chosen to specialize in is a good match. But be honest with yourself. Try and identify the barriers between your current knowledge and the expertise you seek. Ask and answer the questions above. If the answers check out, you have identified a subject you can completely nail. Well done, creativity is coming and your life is going to start seriously rocking.

Does your focus area matter?

Next, you need to consider what your subject area can do for you beyond making you happy. If you are relying on your focus area as your livelihood, then it is important that other people value experts in that particular field. *Doing what you love* sounds dreamy and wonderful but as a career strategy it can seriously tie you into something unprofitable and unappreciated. This is fine if you

---

[21] But in between those years, I tried to become an expert on cloud computing and failed during the seeking stage. Indeed, I've hit Stage 1 for hundreds of subjects, Stage 2 for dozens, Stage 3 for a handful and after that, only software testing, computer security and public speaking have managed to stand the test of time. I expect it will be the same for you do don't get discouraged when you fail one of these tests. Your creativity simply lies elsewhere.

aren't looking for advancement, but if you are, buyer beware.

My own specialty of software testing was great in the 90s when software was shipped on disks and hard to update. Quality had to be baked into a product because software was too expensive to fix after users installed it. Not so much anymore where bugs are easily reported and new versions downloaded automatically. My current specialty, public speaking, wasn't important in the 90s. There were few opportunities to speak on important stages and storytelling wasn't something that pervaded popular culture. Now, however, my classes on storytelling and stage presence are fully booked and I am able to take my message to a worldwide audience. Sometimes timing is everything with the specialty you are pursuing.

So take stock of the industry you work in and understand where the focus area you might adopt fits into the big picture. Is it part of the buzzword nomenclature (like growth hacking, big data, dev ops and so many others are now) or is it a dead end side trail off the critical path? Your ability to be objective about a specialty is important if that specialty is about to become your career. So listen to what's happening in the industry and in the world around you. If you can find something that you can become passionate about and that the world needs, you've got yourself a creative life that also pays the bills. Boo-yah!

Focusing on a single subject that you can master narrows your world and helps you tame a chaotic mind. Specialization is the path to mastery and once you develop expertise, many doors will open for you. The world loves experts and being really good creates a gravity well for opportunity. Being an expert pretty much puts your career on autopilot, but not quite. In the next chapter we'll explore the activities that experts can engage in that take those opportunities to even greater heights.

Focusing on Stage Presence - My Creative Journey Continues

There is a lot to consider when trying to improve your public speaking abilities. How to prepare. How to control anxiety and stage fright. How to begin your presentation. How to modulate the pitch of your voice. When to speak faster and slower. The use of metaphors and oratory technique and all that logos, pathos and ethos stuff. Then there is the conundrum of what to wear, how to act and the whole professionalism thing. It's overwhelming what it takes to be great on stage and the advice out there is mountainous.

So I focused on the aspect of stage presence I found most intriguing: storytelling.

My insight was that if I nailed the stories, both personal and 3rd person, then I could get by with a lot of mistakes everywhere else and people would be likely to forgive me as long as they really enjoyed the stories I told. It would allow me to engage an audience immediately and give me a little more time to learn the rest of my stagecraft.

Turns out I was right. Stories are the best way to make a strong point. They make you human and help you to bring out the humanity in your audience. Stories make you relatable and connect you to your audience in a very powerful way.

I now had a focal point for my learning. As I watched speakers, I honed in on their stories and noticed how those stories were setup and how they were delivered. I got to study the hidden meaning threaded through those stories and when personal details were too much and too little. I noticed that most comedians did nothing but tell stories and that's how they got laughs. I was able to tune out most of the noise from every speaker I watched and focus only on their story. I saw patterns like self-deprecating and never self-congratulating stories. All of this because I was ignoring other aspects of the presentations and focusing on the stories.

This focus greatly accelerated my own ability as a storyteller as I picked stories from my past and began to be mindful of the stories happening in my present. My story collection grew and my skills as a teller increased as I began to seek out ways to practice storytelling. I took up Dungeons &

Dragons[22] again to hone my skills. I worked stories into as many conversations as I could. I began teaching others to tell their stories. I encouraged my kids to tell stories about their day instead of just asking them how their day went. I absorbed the stories happening in and around my life to the point that I saw nothing but stories and storytelling became as natural to me as breathing.

And sure enough, every time I speak I can make 100 mistakes and no one notices because they become absorbed in the power of my story.

Stage 4 Cheat Sheet and Marching Orders:

- Now is the time to play favorites. Pick the subject you are most curious and passionate about and focus on it. You are beginning to become a specialist.

- Make sure you can master it. A specialist is only valuable when they really know a subject well. If you can't learn it to the point of mastery, find something else. The point is to get really good, not just pretty good.

---

[22] This was a two-fer for me. I played the role of Dungeon Master for my then 16-year-old son and a group of his friends. I got to practice storytelling and spend high quality time with my son as he struggled with teenage angst and burgeoning social anxiety. My presence with him at these intensely social events helped him through them. He matured, I matured and we became better friends. What a creative solution... don't you think?

- Watch for instinct begin to emerge. When your brain finds answers so fast that active thought isn't required, you've become a human parallel processor. Expertise is definitely attainable.

- Find every chance you can to wield your expertise. It will only make you better and cement your actions as instincts.

Stage 5: Knowing

When you become an expert, your creativity will accelerate.

Many people are tempted to rest on the knowledge they gained yesterday. They become "good enough" at something and stay that way without trying to push themselves harder. Indeed, the way our school system is set up almost encourages it: learn enough to get a good grade on the exam and then never touch that subject again. We spend the first 20 years of our lives learning and forgetting only to stop learning for good when it is time to go out and earn a living. We separate learning from doing.

What a bad idea. Learning should never stop and that is most especially true for creatives. No matter how much you know about a topic you can always learn more. No matter how complete your knowledge, there are always new insights to be had, connections to be made and corollaries to be investigated. Knowledge is not static. Every day the boundaries of what humankind knows are pushed and information that was once unknown becomes known. Those who stop learning are eventually left behind and become irrelevant. No matter what topic you are trying to master, irrelevance is the only reward if you stop learning. Indeed, even the study of history is clarified by new knowledge.

So knowledge is only the start of the real journey. Rest on what you know now and you'll miss the creativity that will make your life that much better in the future. To nurture your creativity you must always view yourself as a work-in-progress. Be kind to yourself and show some patience. The wait will be worth it.

Einstein embodied this ideal. His expertise kept growing long after he first became really good at physics. It was his vast knowledge and its continual refinement that ultimately spawned his idea for the theory of relativity. A mediocre physicist wouldn't have possessed all the pieces of the space-time puzzle; he would never have been able to connect the various ideas and constructs pieces that led to relativity. It was Einstein's expertise and mastery that led him to be creative.

And still he didn't rest even on such a gargantuan idea. His creative contributions continued as he always saw his last idea as yesterday's news and pushed for more knowledge that would lead him to tomorrow. Einstein continued to crank out mind shattering ideas because he never stopped pushing the boundaries of this knowledge.

I want to encourage you to have the same attitude. That learning never stops. That your last idea is not going to be as good as you next one. The more new knowledge you pile on to your existing knowledge the more creative you will become.

Bill Gates serves as the cautionary tale. His expertise with computers led him to the realization that the operating system was the key to technology dominance. By being an expert he entered a creative realm that even Steve Jobs (who was betting on hardware) didn't manage to summon. But then Gates rested on his original idea whereas Jobs continued to push the boundaries and ended up eclipsing Gates after Windows ran out of steam. It was Jobs who saw mobile coming. Gates missed the mobile era completely because he couldn't see past PCs. His knowledge - and therefore his insight - was tied to a world that had moved past him.

You see, the world won't stop moving and neither can your knowledge. Becoming an expert makes creativity possible but that expertise must be maintained or the creativity is likely to stop. The creative animal must be fed. Let's now turn to its care and feeding.

Expertise creates opportunity, seize it

Remember from the last stage that the more you know about a subject the more insights you develop as your active mind cooperates with your instinctive mind. So once you become an expert, be sure to give yourself time to think, reflect and philosophize to allow this process time to run its course. Put away the selfie sticks. Step back from the shrine to your ego you are building on Facebook. It's time to play the role of expert.

Expertise draws opportunity in and you want to make yourself available to that opportunity because it is very likely to deepen your expertise. One particularly valuable thing expertise brings is fame which attracts people to your gravity well, including other experts with whom you can collaborate and learn from.

Once you become an expert, you automatically become a more interesting person (get used to hearing *wow, you are really good at this!*) and being interesting will pay dividends because people will want to be around you. Being interesting creates its own opportunity because some of the people that are attracted to your particular brand of knowledge are going to be connected to real opportunities. Those people will expand your world by inviting you into theirs. The opportunity they represent will now increase your own knowledge and make you even more valuable.

Expertise creates opportunity directly too, especially if what you know is particularly valuable to a large number of people. People work hard to find experts. They pay a lot to consult with an expert. They go out of their way to hire experts. They are careful to keep experts close. All this means that your expertise will create and maintain opportunities for you and the more impactful your area of expertise is, of course, the more opportunity you'll create.

All of this comes for free when you become an expert. So put yourself out there. Wield your expertise and as you do, watch it grow. And prepare yourself, it's going to be life changing.

Collaborate with other experts

The coming together of two experts is, in a creative sense, a celestial phenomenon. It's rare and wonderful and the magic that happens makes each expert involved that much better, further distancing themselves from the muggles around them. When I began to know a lot of things about software testing in the 90s, I became capable of challenging experts at conferences and online and the ensuing discussion made both myself and the expert I was challenging better.

Avg SAT is based on averages and has a maximum value of 5.0.
Net SAT is calculated based on Overall satisfaction with a maximum value of 200

Evaluation Results

Evaluation Question	Avg. SAT	Net SAT
Overall, I was satisfied with this course.	4.9	186
The instructor consistently linked the course content to Microsoft's business and/or my role.	4.5	166
This course builds skills or knowledge which will improve how I perform my job.	4.8	186
I was provided with the information I needed (logistics, pre-work) for the training in a timely manner.	4.8	182
The classroom setup and hardware (if supplied) functioned appropriately to support face-to-face learning.	4.3	141
The instructor was knowledgeable about the subject matter.	5.0	197
The instructor's presentation skills helped me better understand the content.	4.9	189

Actual results: Evidence of my growing expertise began to come in. The last two lines are the ones that matter most to me. I'm getting good.

Only an expert can challenge another expert because no one else knows enough about a subject to do so. When a non-expert challenges an expert, it is called Q&A and only the non-experts learns from the encounter. But when two experts enter into a discussion, there is the unique opportunity for *both* of them to grow. This is exactly the situation you must seek once you become really good at something. Remember from Stage 1 the idea that *access to experts is the best way to learn?* Well that is still true once you become an expert so stay on the lookout for other experts and when you find one, do both of you a favor by getting to know each other and ensuring that you both grow from the encounter. Hang onto fellow experts, they will will be important companions on this creative journey of yours.

This is exactly why Einstein collaborated with so many other expert physicists. This is why Jimmy Page and Robert Plant/John Lennon and Paul McCartney wrote so many great songs together. Indeed, it is why the best bands of all time are made up of songwriting pairs and band members who are all expert at their specific instrument.[23] Experts make each other better. They push each

---

[23] Led Zeppelin and Rush are two great examples from my generation of musical super groups. Each member of both bands were considered world class with their specific instrument. Both bands were heralded for their creativity and rewarded with a great deal of success. Subpar musicians couldn't have pushed the other members of the band to keep improving. Surround yourself with other experts and your creativity will continue to flourish.

other to places that only another expert is capable of pushing them. When you become an expert, take this to heart and seek out other experts to experience this happy phenomenon for yourself. Don't look at other experts in your field as competition. Look at them as another opportunity to learn.

Dream big, think small

Once you've become an expert, the question now is how to optimize the use of that expertise. As an expert, you have a chance to influence not just your own life and career but the world around you. Here is where most experts differ from ordinary folk. Experts dream big but work small. They never try to "change the world" because all the expertise they've gathered helps them understand just how big and complex the world is and that no single individual or group has much of a chance to actually change it.

That's right, you and your creative ideas aren't going to change the world. Experts may dream big, but they *think* small. They know that to change the world, you have to hack it in some small way and that hack will set the world on a new course that causes the world to change itself.

Think about it for a moment. Of the three companies that have been at the center of "world changing ideas" over the past couple of decades - Microsoft, Google and Apple - none of them have had super big ideas. All they did was hack a world that already existed. Consider:

- Microsoft didn't invent PCs, but what they did was understand that the PC operating system was the key piece of the technology puzzle and the company who owned the OS market would dominate all the other ones. They didn't invent much of anything but they did recognize the most important technology and double down on it. This is creativity! Bill Gates and Paul Allen learned that technology and became expert at its subtleties. Microsoft didn't invent anything new, they just hacked what already existed. That one small hack caused the world to begin to change. That's creativity.

- Google didn't invent search. Yahoo, AltaVista, Lycos and so many others were already there. But Google saw what the others didn't: a growing web was making discoverability really hard. They came in with a new way to determine search result relevance, one small piece of the information retrieval field. This is not a big idea at all, only a small a hack. Again, the hack didn't change the world, it simply provided the key piece of the puzzle that caused the world to change itself. Google's insight caused that to happen. That's creativity.

- Apple didn't invent the MP3 player or the smartphone. Indeed, they were very late to both of those games and far behind industry leaders like Blackberry, Windows CE and the Palm Pilot. However, they foresaw the key problem that eluded the big players: that no one was developing apps for mobile because they were too hard to find, install and configure. The app store solved that problem and attracted developers who then helped changed the world. Small idea, big change. That's creativity.

You may not be able to change the world but you can point the world in the right direction. Experts are the ones who do this because in their field of expertise they have the knowledge of all the moving pieces. It's knowledge that is the key differentiator between a leader and a trailer, between an agent of change and a follower of rules. But that knowledge has to be acted upon, which each of these companies did. The moment Microsoft knew the world was going to revolved around PCs was the moment that the small idea - the hack - mattered most. The moment Google knew the world would revolve around the web was the moment their search relevance tweak won the day. When the world started revolving around mobile, Apple was there with the app store.

But knowledge is not static. Microsoft won the desktop then lost the web. Google won the web then lost mobile. Apple won mobile and will likely lose the internet of things. Knowing is a great thing, but you have to keep learning or the world will move past you. Following from this, expertise is therefore also not static. Never stop thinking. Never stop learning and seek the small hacks that will keep you on top of your game and guide the world around you instead of allowing the world to guide you through it.

Knowing Stage Presence - My Creative Journey Culminates

My search for another stage presence expert to accelerate my own growing expertise began at conferences watching other presenters. If you've ever been to conferences hearing so-called "professional speakers," you will understand what a frustrating experience this was. The number of people who are really good on stage are rare. My quest was a long one.

When I finally did begin interacting with other people really good at their craft, my engagement with them was equally frustrating. Too many of them were hesitant to engage with me. I have little patience for people who don't want to grow and be challenged. Beware of people who think they have it all figured out or are afraid they will be outshone by another expert. Those people have plateaued and make unlikely companions to the realms beyond expertise (yes, there is more creativity to be had beyond expertise as we shall see in Stages 6 and 7). It is never the case that you will be "best" at anything. Whatever you are trying to become, embracing others who are also good at it will make you better. I was trying to be *an* expert, not *the* expert.

In fact, it was on this journey that I began to appreciate diversity from a completely different viewpoint. If I was going to find an expert to collaborate with, why not one with a completely different background and set of experiences? Indeed, what could another white dude in his 40s teach this white dude in his 40s? Maybe there was something I was missing *because* I was a 40-something white dude interacting with other 40-something white dudes.

This was the insight that made me approach conferences differently. I began seeking out female speakers and those of color and lifestyles different than my own. The more their background was different than mine, the harder I worked to engage them in conversation. Finally, I had a strategy that narrowed the field and it began to work for me.

Learn to seek out different perspectives and to appreciate the delightful variety of people and opinions this world has to offer. Those perspectives deepen your own expertise faster than working with people who look and think like you do.

My ultimate success came in the form of one Michelle Dickinson (@medickinson), a woman a decade or so my junior with a completely different racial profile and geographic experiences than my own. Her stage presence was powerful and her perspective was fresh. Finally, I found another expert who could teach me something and vice-versa.

Now getting her to collaborate was actually an easy task. Unlike stage 1 where there is a huge mismatch between your expertise and that of your mentor, two experts have a lot in common. It actually took nothing more than a few emails and tweets back and forth to establish the idea of doing a talk together. Once we both got excited about the idea, the *expert effect* - that accelerated learning that two experts experience when working together - took over. When that happened we were both highly incented to follow through and on April 5, 2015 we "rocked the stage" together in Auckland, New Zealand and both of us came away even more expert in our craft.[24]

In fact, only a month or so after we rocked the stage together, I began to get standing ovations for my talks. My collaboration with Michelle set off a firestorm of creative energy that moved me to a new level of skill and capability. Only another expert could have taken me to that level.

Never look at other experts as competition. They are no such thing. Indeed, they are your ticket to a whole new level of mind expansion. There is indeed a place beyond expertise and only another expert can get you there.

---

[24] You can see the result of our collaboration here:
https://www.youtube.com/watch?v=uKtMwmWv6Q0.

Stage 5 Cheat Sheet and Marching Orders:

- Take advantage of the opportunities your expertise delivers. They are ways to practice your growing expertise and cement it in your mind.

- Seek out other experts and use them to get better yourself (while simultaneously making them better too). When possible, choose diversity over someone just like you. A different, expert perspective will help you grow.

- Think small. Mind the gap between how the world works and the way it should work. Fill those gaps and you've just used your creativity to hack the world.

Stage 6: Creating

Creativity isn't a talent; it's a lifestyle. Begin living that lifestyle now.

Knowing your stuff and carefully nurturing that knowledge makes creativity possible. This next stage is where your creativity finally makes its impact on your life. But it isn't enough that creativity appear now and again with random bolts of deep insight. A true creative doesn't have to wait for ideas but can reliably summon them at will.

I have found over the course of my creative life that my creativity has four distinct drivers, a quadrilateral of sorts with each corner containing a cache of sustenance for my creativity. At times when I need (or just want) to be creative I will stroll through the four corners of this quad looking for inspiration and wisdom. These four places are each powerful so we'll take them in turn and discuss each in some depth. But as a foursome, they are indeed fearsome and putting them *all* into practice in whatever mix makes the most sense for you will help nurture and maximize your creative potential.

Don't rush through this chapter! As you read about my creative drivers, I want you to pause and contemplate your own. I suspect they are already present in your life and you just need to shine a light on them as I have done. So get your flashlight app ready, we're going to illuminate some parts of your life and those parts are going to begin to become really important to you as they work to drive you to new creative heights.

Find your center

Being centered is incredibly helpful for your creative processes. Few people could be creative strapped to a train track. It's not a place conducive to being receptive to good ideas. You'd be too alert for the sounds of an oncoming train, too worried about your predicament. Of course, this is an extreme example, but you get my point. I bet you can name the places where productivity is problematic for you fairly readily: for me it's noisy shopping malls, day care centers (or around kids who are doing anything except sleeping), schools, libraries (yep, tried it... artificial silence is just too weird for me), government buildings, crowded streets and did I mention shopping?

Identify your creative kryptonite so that you understand the places to avoid when you need creativity. It is also a good exercise in mindfulness, which you will need to identify the places you *can* be creative in.

Understand that I am making a distinction between creativity and productivity here. I can be productive on a plane, just not creative. I fly a great deal and get tons of work done but I am rarely creative. Same for coffee shops and restaurants. In fact, I've become hypersensitive to where I am when I have ideas and the activities that help start my creative biorhythms. I'm now asking you to put some thought into these places so you can turn to them when you need creative time.

The first creative sanctuary I ever noticed was way back when I was in my teens: washing my car. The reason for this isn't something I've spent a lot of time pondering. But I do enter some sort of creative trance when I am washing my car. I don't really care *why* I am creative, only that I am. It's certainly not because it's outdoors because I can give my car a sponge bath inside my garage in the middle of winter listening to the White Stripes with the same creative output as washing it on a sunny day in my backyard to the tune of birdsong. Perhaps it has something to do with the finely detailed, methodical process of wash, dry, buff. Perhaps it is the constant movement of my body that makes my mind become more active. I truly don't know. I also don't really care. Fact is, I have a ton of great ideas while I am washing my car which explains why my car is almost always clean. I cherish my ideas and my creative space, the clean car is just a side-effect of that.

In order to find your own spot, you have to train yourself to notice your creative activity. My car washing insight came as a result of a few particularly exciting Dungeons & Dragons games I designed for my gaming group when I was a teenager. Whenever I turned my mind toward D&D while washing my car I designed really exciting encounters and my group had a ton of fun. I noticed the pattern and then integrated car washing into my preparation routine.[25]

Knowing when creativity might make an appearance allows you to lay out a welcome mat for it. Take stock of your creative moments. Be aware of what you are doing when a creative idea strikes. Where are you? What activity are you involved in? What time of the day is it? What were you thinking about when the idea struck?

The theory[26] is that creativity has triggers and incubators that coax it into appearing when you need it. Recreate those triggers as often as you can and track your success rate. Monitor this process carefully and you have the makings of your very own creative ritual that will make you centered and help you summon creativity on demand.

---

[25] Decades later one of my players endorsed me on LinkedIn for my Dungeon Master skills. Turns out creativity doesn't just get you noticed. It makes you memorable.

[26] A wonderfully readable study detailing the rituals of some of the most creative people in history can be found at http://www.infowetrust.com/creative-routines/.

Over the years I have established my own set of creative rituals. I noticed early on in my career that my best ideas come in the morning and evening and less so in the afternoon so I have established my productivity routines around doing the more mundane work like editing, polishing and debugging in the afternoon and saved my productive times for writing, coding, storytelling and other creative work. If I have to be creative in the afternoon, I am better off at a crowded pub or brewery where the noise and the smell of beer distracts me from boredom. The only way you can learn your own creative times and establish rituals as triggers for great ideas is to be mindful of where and when your creative juices are flowing.

My morning coffee times and evening beer times are the moments where I have had the most ideas that have led to new papers, presentations, products and patents. If I need to be creative, I frame my day around those times: I get up early and stay home in the morning, pounding coffee and enjoying the peace and quiet; then I go to the office to pay my dues and execute on other people's priorities; then on the way home I stop by a brewery for some additional me-time. These are my very favorite days! I expect to be creative and am rarely disappointed. My routine has become a reliable way to loosen the creative flow in my mind. When I want to be creative, I know exactly what, when, where and how to make it happen. That needs to be your goal right now: start being mindful of your creative-what, -when, -why and -how.

While you are watching your own life for signs of creativity, don't forget to listen to others as well. Life will often speak to you through the people you are closest to. In fact, it was my daughter who pointed out that my backyard hot tub was a creative place for me. I had been retreating to that warm, wet sanctuary for what I thought was peace and quiet but she noticed my thoughtfulness after I emerged from it and my tendency to gravitate to pen/paper or laptop immediately afterward. Her simple comment *aww, dad found his happy place!* was the clue I needed to understand that the number of places I can retreat to in order to stir my creative juices had just grown by one.[27]

So... what are your creative spots? Work to identify the places that make you feel centered and then hang out there as often as you need to be creative. Once you identify your center, both the places and the activities that focus your mind, go there and wait for the release your creativity. You aren't likely to be disappointed with the result.

Understand your distractions

The human brain is a pretty chaotic place where uncertainty, anxiety and self-doubt like to party.

---

[27] Spa vendors will cite research about hydrotherapy increasing the oxygen flow to the brain as health reasons for using a hot tub. Maybe this explains why I have such good ideas in mine. Maybe it explains why many people have good ideas in the shower. I do not know and really don't care. They fact that it is a creative place for me is all that really matters.

Any of these are very, very bad for your creativity so it's good to have a set of activities that allow you to interrupt those processes and reset your creative ability. I call such purposeful interruptions *distractions*.

Distractions are activities that divert your attention away from your own internal conversation. In general, they are powerful enough to "take you away" to another place imaginary or real. Distraction helps your mind by changing the focus from one part of the brain to another. It assists your creativity by giving the creative parts of your mind time to rest while exercising other parts that have no role in your creative moments.

Activities like meditation, reading, lovemaking, watching a movie and the like have this effect for some people. These activities remove you from reality and prevent your mind from reveling in anxiety and depression. Or, they can just give the creative parts of your mind a rest.

It is good for your mind to get distracted like this. You can't be always-on; it is just not the way the human mind is wired. Some brains respond to rest and some to strenuous activity. Some respond to music or art, while others to gaming, sex, meditation or even quiet contemplation. By embracing a variety of distractions you can begin to recognize which ones your own brain responds to so when you need a break aimed at sparking your creativity, you know what will work. Be mindful of the activities that reset your brain and go to them when you need them.

My distraction is live music, which - once again - I noticed because part of the lifestyle of a creative is being mindful of your intellectual biorhythms. There are patterns to your creativity but you have to be looking for them. My creativity spikes the day after I watch live music. There is something about the complete visual and auditory sensory overload. There is something about the feeling of the sound waves booming through my body and the camaraderie of sharing in primordial screams and communal singalongs with complete strangers that resets my mind. What a gift that I know this! I can retreat to my local music parlor to receive this most sacred of intellectual sacraments.

I discovered this distraction the same way you will discover yours: by being mindful of my creative moments and then reverse engineering them to their cause. The day after I listen to live music my work is better, my ideas stronger and my mood higher.

My other distraction (yes I feel lucky for having two!) is being onstage. For whatever reason, I cannot carry my cares and worries to the stage. For whatever reason, I completely let go and surrender to the energy of the crowd. When I give a talk my mind is fully engaged. My bond with the audience becomes stronger as my presentation progresses. My thought processes become completely wrapped up in the current moment. I come off the stage a new man.

Why this happens is far less important than that it *does indeed happen*. A bad day or a bumpy personal life can both be set aside, and sometimes completely cured, by getting onstage and giving a presentation. I can't believe I used to cancel talks if I was having a bad day. Now I go out of my way to schedule one. That's how powerful a distraction it is for me.

How about for you? This is a question that needs an answer. Your life is likely to be much better if you can control your own mind with on demand distractions.

Know your inspirations

There is a reason that people make motivational posters. They sell. It is a natural state of the human condition to strive for self-improvement and motivating yourself to do more with your life is a common theme in both our work and personal lives. Having said that, I do not own any motivational posters.

Instead, I get my motivation from other people. Actual humans who are really good at the things I want to get good at inspire me. People who have mastered the things that I want to master help inform my own path and provide confidence that my goal is actually obtainable. If Ron White can slay an audience, then why can't I?

86

My inspirations stand as proof that what I want to achieve is possible and that regular humans like me can be creative and accomplish amazing things. Sometimes those inspirations are superheroes like Martin Luther King, Jr and Winston Churchill whose speeches I often use as inspiration when I am preparing for a big presentation. But mostly they are ordinary people whose lives range from spikes of brilliance to consistent common wisdom. Writers like Bob Lefsetz, Dona Sarkar, Ron Judd (aka Mr. Wrap) and Sam Harris are better at their craft than I am and when writer's block inevitably hits, I seek out their work as inspiration. If I am struggling with some aspect of a speech, it is the TED talks of Michelle Dickinson or Amanda Palmer I will watch. If I feel like a talk needs to be more serious, it's Carl Sagan I turn to. When humor is necessary it is Mitch Hedburg or Ron White who get my attention. When profundity is required then Neil De Grasse Tyson and John Oliver are my go-to guys.

Who are your inspirations? Don't take on life all by yourself. It's too much work to face it alone. Whether your inspirations are people you can actually interact with or only learn from remotely, they can supply you with energy, inspiration and the confidence that what you want to accomplish is possible.

Finally, make sure you pick a set of inspirations from a variety of people. Choose people of different genders, backgrounds, ethnicities and lifestyles. The diversity of thought and ideas will help push your thinking to places it wouldn't go if you only chose to learn from people who are just like you.

Seek out stillness and solitude

Finally, the power of stillness is something we've lost in recent decades as the noise of the outside world fills our lives through the screens we carry around wherever we go. Look around you in restaurants, bars, airports and waiting rooms. Everyone is staring at a screen of some sort. Screens bringing a constant barrage of information and other people's priorities to minds that are finding it increasingly hard to settle.

Make time for stillness in your life. Embrace the strange satisfaction that is silence and welcome those times when you just sit and observe and let your environment dictate what your mind sees. Put your phone away and just sit dead still and let your mind go where it wants. Let thoughts come and go. Don't force anything. Your brain can become like murky water and sometimes it just needs to rest so the haze can settle to the bottom and a clearer mind can emerge. Give yourself 30 minutes a day. Increase it if necessary. What's more important, that Facebook post of someone you barely know lying about how cool their life is... or the continued functioning of your own wonderfully creative mind? If it is the former, please return this book, I have nothing further to offer you except my pity and I'll give you that for free.

Creating Stage Presence - My Creative Destination

In October of 2015 I was asked by my CEO and head of Human Resources to create a presentation called "A Growth Mindset at Microsoft." *James, they asked, please make it so that it doesn't sound like corporate Kool-Aid.* You see my reputation as a wise, straight-talking speaker and presenter had already grown to the top echelon the company. Even before you reach true expertise, you become a lot better than the people around you and that has the effect of generating some notoriety.

Of course I told them that I could even though the honest truth was that I had no idea what a growth mindset was and, frankly, it was the sort of nonsense that sounded *exactly* like corporate Kool-Aid! But I knew that I had creativity on my side and could summon it at will. My confidence in nailing this task was very, very high. I invoked my creative routine and went to work. I spent an evening listening to live music and resetting my brain. The next morning, I put my creative process in action. Here's how it went down.

My process starts the night before I need to be creative by readying my workspace. Now I have a beautiful home office I purpose built for working. In it are all the things I find interesting and soothing, but this is not the space I actually work in. Turns out that I've never had a single good idea in my purpose-built home office. Instead, my creative space is my comfy chair in the family room of my house. Why? Because I've never had a good idea in my office and I have them regularly in my comfy chair. I've learned not to question why but it doesn't keep me from lamenting the fact that my lovingly decorated office is not a place conducive to my creative process.

Next, my creative morning starts early for me because I have a lot of ideas in the morning. I get up at 5, make coffee and settle in for a morning of creating. In fact, my entire talk was created that morning and puzzled over in the early afternoon as I washed my car. When I delivered it later that same afternoon I got a standing ovation at the end. Proof that my creativity is there for me and that my routine works.

Stage 6 Cheat Sheet and Marching Orders:

- Find your center. Be mindful of the places where your creative ideas come and return to the places where your best ideas occur.

- Understand your distractions. The things that help jostle your thought process are the things that will reset your mind and prepare it to be creative.

- Know your inspirations. The people, places and things that make you see the beauty and goodness in the world will make you strive that much harder to achieve them.

- Seek out solitude. Give your mind time to rest. Put away the screens and focus on your own thoughts and needs.

- Build your creative routine. Each of the above needs to be part of a creative routine you execute whenever you need that most holy of sacraments. Daily, weekly or whenever you need to be creative... you will be able to because your routine will trigger your mind to create.

Stage 7: Living

Once you have achieved a creative life there is only one thing left to do. Live it.

In a world of instant information, it is easy to forget your creativity. With answers to any question only a few clicks away it's easy to let your creativity atrophy because so many decisions can be made with the help of one of those screens on your desk, in your backpack or in your hand. A thinking, active mind just isn't a requirement for modern life.

This final stage of creativity is about not allowing that to happen. It's about embracing life and your ability to create things that improve yours. No screen can be a substitute for actual life and it is in living in the real world where our creativity flourishes. It is in the real world where stories, experiences and inspiration are found. This final stage is about everyday practices you can use to ensure that learning, thinking, seeking, focusing, knowing and creating are regular cycles that you perform on a variety of people, places and experiences throughout your life. That's right, just because you've gotten to the final stage doesn't mean it's over. In fact, you are just getting started!

This last stage is about repeating the prior stages and reminding yourself that you are never really fully formed as a creative being. No matter how old or experienced, your creative life is ready to be renewed and now that you know how to be creative, the fun has only just begun. Indeed, one of the joys of aging is that creativity is still spread out before you, and - because of your wealth of experiences with wielding it - it is more accessible than ever.

So now put the creative lifestyle into practice. This final stage is about living the lifestyle of a creative and making creativity a matter of habit and routine. It means asking your own questions and forming your own answers. There is a level of mindfulness that creative people adopt with respect to living their lives that you should consider making your own. Creative people are intensely aware of the people around them and the activities in which they are engaged. The idea is very much that creatives are *always* on the alert for inspiration. We are always on the prowl for ideas to ponder and hacks that will make our lives or the world around us better in some way.

Learn something from everyone you meet

The first thing you need to understand about living a creative lifestyle is that creatives engage more profoundly with other people than non-creatives. People, as the most complex neurological organism on the planet, represent the best chance to challenge our ideas and provide a spark for our creativity. As such they are the obvious source of interest for the creative mind. I'm suggesting you put this into practice with a simple life hack that I think you'll enjoy: *try to learn something from everyone you meet.*

Think about it for a moment. The best human interactions aren't the bored, can't-wait-for-this-person-to-leave meetings. They are the times when the conversation is lively and the connection is intense and authentic. These are the times where you make new friends and maybe even fall in love a little bit. You can greatly increase the chances of these kinds of interactions by focusing on the other person with more energy than you have for anything else (at least at that moment). I've experimented with a number of ways to do this (because, yes, I get bored with people really easily and need something concrete to center on or my mind will stray[28]) and found what I call *active learning* to be the solution. I actively try to learn something from everyone I meet.

When you are focused on learning something from people you meet, you listen more intently and engage more fully into their presence and the conversation you are sharing. People recognize

---

[28] I actually dozed off in a one-on-one with one of my direct reports once. How embarrassing for me and insulting to her. Now my focus is much better with my practice of more active learning. Trying to learn something from everyone I meet has amplified my ability to concentrate so that this doe.

this and appreciate your engagement. My theory is that they open up more and share more and it is in this additional information exchange that you might find that something they have to teach you. At the very least, they walk away with a more positive impression of you and your willingness to engage with them. Furthermore, if they truly have nothing to offer, you get to this conclusion more quickly and can move on to someone with whom you might have a more powerful creative connection.[29]

It's great mindfulness practice to approach every human encounter with the goal of learning something. I've found it also somehow increases the *humanness* of the interaction because once I find a subject of mutual interest I can ask questions that encourage the other person to divulge their feelings and opinions about the topic we are discussing, thus getting to know that person, their interests and their lives on a much deeper level than would have otherwise happened.

What you are doing here is essentially putting all the people in your life in the role of teacher and mentor. There is something intensely gratifying about teaching someone something. So feel good

---

[29] My most intense relationships are with those friends with whom I have a creative connection. For me collaborating on a creative endeavor is the height of human encounter and the bonds forged during creative connections are much stronger than bonds of simple fun. I suspect that most creatives share this worldview and insist that their lives are spent with other creative souls.

about yourself because you just provided someone with that gift by being their student! It's like giving a little piece of yourself to another person and finding that they cherish it. This is what makes the teacher-and-willing-student relationship so gratifying in both directions: each person involved both gives and receives and there is no better way to ensure that both enjoy and want to continue that kind of a relationship. After all, both parties are benefitting.

Remember from stage 1 that access to experts is the best way to learn? Since experts often don't look or talk any different than regular people the only way to really discover what someone has to teach you is to look for it. I believe going into every human encounter with the default goal of learning something from them will help you identify your life teachers' faster than nearly anything else.

Add a creative side hustle

I made the point in the opening chapter that we were born curious and inquisitive and it is schools and social conventions that drove that curiosity out of us. We can't let our creativity go so easily and without a fight. We need some kind of creative activity in our lives lest we risk creative atrophy. Enter the side hustle - something you are engaged with inside or outside your day job that satisfies your creative need. One way to do this is to make sure you are engaged in *something*, really anything, creative.

The first place to look are all the tasks you are involved in anyway. Ask yourself is there part of your job that is creative? Or at least more creative than any other part? Is there a way to focus more on that part of your work than the others? Might you be able to add other creative tasks to your day and delegate some that are not?

If you can turn your day job into a more creative endeavor, then that is the best possible outcome. This way you can't really avoid creativity because it is part of your workday. But if you can't find anything creative about your actual day job, then my recommendation is to adopt a side hustle outside your job that is creative. What can you build, brew, draw, code, cook, photograph, design, paint, teach, write, choreograph, cartoon, play, film, etc., that will reintroduce you to the creative world and either keep or start your juices flowing?

If creativity is lacking in your life, add it back in intentionally and spend as much time as you can going through the stages of learning, thinking, seeking, focusing, knowing, creating. Then rinse and repeat until something sticks. Remember, learning is a lifelong activity; you could and should repeat this cycle hundreds of times over the course of your life. Sometimes getting only to Stage 1 or 2 and other times higher up the chain. You never really know until you try and when you begin to climb into the creative realms, you are going to want to linger there.

What a great life you have ahead of you!

Embrace the creativity around you

Another way to add a little creativity to your day is to embrace the creativity that is already present in the world. Understand that as you progress through the stages of creativity that others have been there before you. By paying attention to those creatives and their creations you are inspiring your own creativity and doing a huge favor for your life. Look to other creatives to remind you of your own creative possibilities.

In my life, I enjoy being profound from time to time. I go out of my way to listen to the Martin Luther King Jr's of the world, absorbing wisdom like *I have a dream that one day my four little children will not be judged by the color of their skin but by the content of their character.* I often wondered how creative people came up with such beautiful and profound statements. But the more I sought out such wisdom, the more it started happening to me. That's right, by surrounding myself with profundity I absorbed it and became profound myself.

It began with clever little insights and witty remarks and ended with widely retweeted comments like *software is the opposable thumb of the human mind* and *serendipity is nothing more than fate trying not to be noticed.*[30] As I embraced profundity in my own life, profundity began to

---

[30] Take a look at my Twitter feed (www.twitter.com/@docjamesw) and scroll for a while. Once profundity takes hold, it flows freely.

embrace me (see, I just did it again). This realization has led me to seek out profundity wherever I can find it, be it in satirical cartoons in newspapers or shows like *Last Week Tonight* with John Oliver. Simply being around such creativity will ensure that some of it rubs off.

This is why you find creatives in places like art shows and museums. We use other people's creativity to recharge our own. So if satire is your thing, seek out the satirical people and when you find them follow their work. The internet makes this really easy. If poetry is your thing, steep yourself in the poetry of others and use it to inspire your own. Whatever your art, there are others practicing it too and making their creativity part of your everyday routine will keep the creative lifestyle close... which is exactly what living a creative life is all about. It means not accepting the world created by others. It means wanting and then demanding and then creating more for yourself. It means that instead of life dragging you along where it will, you decide where you want your life to go. Take control.

And it is with this thought that I leave you to your own creative devices. But before we bid farewell I have included next some of my more popular blog posts which touch on creative subjects. They didn't really fit in the body of the book but they are part of my creative body of work nonetheless. I hope you enjoy them.

Never stop creating.

Living Stage Presence - The Journey Never Ends

As soon as I became really good onstage, amazing things began to happen in my mind *as I was presenting*. I shouldn't have been surprised that my journey came full circle, because I have made the point over and over that creativity is a journey without a destination.

I realized that my expertise on stage began to become rote. Without any preparation at all, I could get up and give a compelling talk on almost any subject. At the same time my mind began to roam free because stage presence had become an instinct. I was able to both present and create, coming up with lines like *software is the opposable thumb for the human mind* **while** I was onstage. Spontaneous creativity without preparation or active thought. This is the reward for living a creative lifestyle. I am now increasing my creativity just by getting up onstage. What a crazy benefit and one that I did not see coming.

Indeed, I've added the stage as one of my centered places alongside washing my car and soaking in my hot tub and I've added it as a distraction alongside live music. If I am having a bad day, speaking banishes it. If I am stuck on a topic, all I have to do is give a presentation about it. And, of course, audiences are easy to find because my reputation as a speaker has grown because of my expertise.

If there is any additional proof you need, come find me on a stage somewhere. Watch me walk the talk you've just spent so many hours reading.

Live long and... create.

Stage 7 Cheat Sheet and Marching Orders:

- Treat everyone you meet as a potential creative mentor and try to learn something from each and every human encounter.

- Start a creative side hustle that will help to reawaken your creative self.

- Embrace your art. Others are good at it too. Let them into your life to inspire you to bigger and more creative things.

Appendices

What follows are posts from the author that relate to the subject of learning, mindfulness, self-improvement and creativity all gathered in one place to take advantage of the momentum you now have in pursuing creativity.

And don't stop there. Docjamesw.com has pointers to the authors other books, papers and slide decks along with the hidden link

www.docjamesw.com/the-7-stages-of-creativity/

that is only given to people who possess this book.

Enjoy!

Just Suck Less

Because 'just be yourself' is the worst advice ever.

It's the advice we hear more often than any other. *Just be yourself* is its own meme. It is the go-to counsel from shrinks' couches to social media. It's the meaningless tripe we tell our kids when we send them out into the world or say to a colleague before a big interview. We have to stop this self-satisfied, grossly narcissistic practice which, by definition, is the worst advice ever.

Being yourself means dropping your guard. It means allowing your fear, anxiety and prejudices to manifest upon the world. It means licking your plate at a restaurant or publicly scratching that itch without regard to its location. Being yourself is what you do when you are alone in a hotel room and no one wants to see that shit. Being yourself is something none of us ever actually do and if you think you are doing it, then you have far too high an opinion of yourself and you need this article more than anyone else.

Imagine what would happen if every racist, bigot, extremist and self-righteous dickhead would stop being themselves. This world would become a much better place instantaneously. Here's my idea, instead of being yourself, *try being someone better than you.*

Being yourself means eschewing growth. It means stagnation. Truth is, none of us are good enough to just be ourselves. When, instead, you try being someone better than you, the possibility of personal growth occurs. Imagine, for a moment, a large population of people intent not on being themselves but on being someone better. How cool would that be?

But being better is vague. Being better is open-ended and makes it too easy to disappoint yourself. So, as an alternative, I recommend approaching every situation simply trying to *just suck less.*

Begin by being mindful of your suck-i-ness. When you suck out loud remember it and next time you are in a similar situation, consciously remove that suck-age from the scenario.

Guess what? You just sucked less! Continue in this manner by sucking less in a second situation and then a third. Eventually, sucking less will become a habit and your overall ability to suck will become greatly diminished.

Go about your daily activities on the alert for suck-age. Do not allow your suck-age to hide behind your ego or your prejudices. Shine a light on that shit; call it out and label it. That way the next time suck begins to rear its head you can do the exact opposite of 'just be yourself' and, instead, be someone who sucks less than you.

As you master this, create an anti-suck sphere-of-influence by passing around this *suck less* advice whenever you can. Send your kids off to school with an admonition to *suck a little less today sweetheart!* Suggest to that colleague going into a meeting with his VP to *suck less dude!* Here's an idea for that presentation: *suck less!* It's good advice for your commute and the work product you create. It's a handy cheat sheet for every personal interaction throughout your day. It's as helpful in the checkout line as it is when adding a tip to the bill. And for all you holiday shoppers out there, this year let's all try to make it... everybody say it with me now... *suck less!*

One day you may awake to a world that sucks a little less. You may come to realize that much of your own ability to suck has been removed from your day to day activities. Then, maybe, just maybe, you will finally have earned the right to just be yourself.

Still, just to be sure, keep that shit confined to your hotel room just in case you missed a spot.

The Power of Procrastination

I was always a decent student; it wasn't until I learned to procrastinate that I started to excel.

You read that right. Procrastination is the harbinger of creativity; the provider of insight. It is often the difference between success and mediocrity. Had I not learned to procrastinate, indeed, to turn procrastination into an art form, I would not be where I am today. Procrastination can take credit for my PhD. Procrastination made me an executive at Google. Procrastination is the reason I have the word 'Distinguished' in my Microsoft title.

Procrastination isn't just not bad. It's the most underrated modern career skill out there and those who fail to embrace it, or worse, spend time berating themselves for it, will have a tougher climb to the top. The modern world is no place for the over prepared and meticulously organized. The world you think you are preparing for will have changed into something else long before you are finished preparing for it. The work you are organizing so obsessively will be irrelevant before it is fully organized. There is too much to know now and more things to know are springing up constantly. How can anyone navigate this world of knowledge overload?

The answer lies in procrastination and how it trains you to know only what you need to know only for the time you need to know it. Procrastination is the just-in-time preparation strategy for a just-in-time world. And lest you fear you are arriving late to the procrastination bandwagon, relax. That's the great thing about procrastination, whatever time you have remaining is the exact amount of time you need.

Procrastination creates pressure

People who don't procrastinate live in a fairy world. They plan ahead. They organize their notes after every lecture and pursue action items after every meeting. Homework is completed far in advance and life progresses with a predictability that, well, just isn't real. Failure to procrastinate is tantamount to rejecting the world as it actually exists.

You see, homework isn't assigned in the real world. You don't get advance notice of when things are due. Deadlines pop up without announcing themselves. There are market pressures, competitive pressures, personal pressures, team dynamics, technology glitches and any number of things that make preparation either impossible or a huge waste of time. You either drive yourself crazy preparing for everything or you learn to deal with the pressure created by the uncontrollable and the unforeseen.

Procrastination creates artificial pressure which trains you to deal with real pressure during your career. Every good job and most of the decent ones are performed under pressure. Procrastinators become familiar with pressure. They learn to expect its presence and treat it as just another variable to consider. Procrastinators learn to control panic. They are rarely surprised and develop improvisational skills the envy of any actor. Embrace the life of a procrastinator so you too can develop this keen ability to perform under pressure.

Procrastination requires prioritization

People who don't procrastinate have more time to learn. This extra time means they can get more of a subject into their head than procrastinators who, by definition, wait too long to learn any subject completely. Simply put, people who don't procrastinate learn more.

Learning more necessarily means learning things that don't matter. It means spending time on things that are important and things that are not as important. People who don't procrastinate don't have to differentiate between the two. They have time to learn it all, or at least most of it. So they end up filling up valuable neural real estate on things that just don't matter.

But the procrastinator has the advantage of a compressed time schedule and this means they have no choice but to prioritize. The procrastinator is forced to focus on only the most important parts of any subject. The procrastinating brain doesn't have to make room for the unimportant stuff and can use its full capacity to learn all the really necessary parts more completely. It is only through thorough and repeated procrastination that one masters this prioritization.

The ability to pick apart a problem and find its most important parts is a crucial modern career skill. Procrastinating is a great way to obtain this skill and teaches us to learn the important parts of any subject first.

Procrastination promotes insight

People who don't procrastinate aren't incentivized to create shortcuts. Why bother when you have so much time on your hands? Procrastinators, however, feel this shortcut incentive strongly and it creates perfect conditions for insight to flourish.

My own procrastination led to an insight that regularly had me racking up 'A' grade after 'A' grade with mere minutes on the hour for study time. My goal was simple: study only the material that was likely to be on the exam. My insight was that two factors indicate topic's likelihood of landing on an exam: the amount of time a professor spends lecturing on that topic and the amount of interest the professor displays during those lectures. Topics that got a lot of air time and that were delivered with some enthusiasm would feature prominently on exams. Of course, the same can be said of the corporate worker. The things the CEO talks about most and displays the most enthusiasm for are important. Working on things important to the CEO is really good for your career.

This strategy honed my power of prioritization, focused my cram time and provided a systematic way to study the material at hand. If there is one thing a procrastinator is good at, it's coming up with a system.

Knowing what to study was only the beginning. Instead of just poring over the material trying to cram it into my head, I went through it and created exam questions of my own. More often than not I could get close enough to the actual exam questions to give me a decided advantage over even the staunchest non-procrastinator. After the exam, of course, procrastinator and non-procrastinator alike would forget large volumes of information (why we insist on teaching students things they don't need to know isn't tackled here). It's just that the stuff I forgot was all important enough to justify its temporary neural real estate. Whereas much of the stuff the non-procrastinators forgot never needed to be learned in the first place.

Now who is the time waster here? Certainly not the procrastinator.

Procrastination saves time

Cram time is the best time to study simply because it is last minute and there is no time to forget anything. Nor is there any need to re-study anything you committed to memory days or weeks earlier because you didn't know anything days or weeks earlier. That was when you were procrastinating!

Procrastination means that your knowledge is fresh. That new-car smell is still wafting around your tidy and uncluttered frontal lobe. The pages of your books and notes will be fresh in your memory ready to be recalled during the exam. When the inevitable post-exam knowledge flush occurs there is no reason to be sentimental about it because it was more of a one night stand with that knowledge rather than a proper relationship.

Procrastination is the preparation ritual

Study rituals among non-procrastinators often start weeks in advance. Rewriting notes, re-doing homework, making flash cards and rereading chapters puts the mind on notice much as pre-game rituals put an athlete's muscles on notice. The message: it's almost game time!

This is another huge advantage for procrastinators. We put our brains on notice much closer to game time. Our brains don't have to anticipate game days for days or weeks in advance. Such a prolonged ritual is tiring. The anticipation is stressful. The adrenaline and passion is harder to maintain over such a stretch of time. Procrastinators follow much closer to the athlete model where maximum alertness is obtained right when you need it most, just as you enter the field of play.

Procrastination is the ritual. It eases the mind into its game day ritual so that it is ready when the starting whistle blows.

In Parting

Over the course of your lifetime you will learn and forget vast volumes of information. You will acquire and later release reams of knowledge. Much of what you are learning now will not be useful tomorrow. This is the world that exists today. Denying this reality will make success that much harder.

Ensuring that you learn the most impactful things and know them at the most important times is what will make you successful. Procrastination is the path to prioritizing what you need to know and retaining it for the time period in which you need to know it.

What are you waiting for? Start procrastinating today.

On Underachievement

Imagine a world where everyone was qualified for what they do. By not aiming too high, we may find where we were really meant to be.

If you are not meant to be a doctor yet attempt to become one because of societal treatment, parental pressure or personal whim it's very doubtful you will be a good one. You might fail in the attempt, or succeed in the attempt only to be a marginal success. The world needs extraordinary doctors, no sane person wants to be treated by an ordinary one. So if you are ordinary do yourself and the rest of us a favor and stay out of the medical profession, or if you do enter it please aim low and leave the really important stuff to those who are more gifted.

This may seem harsh, but there is opportunity written all over it for those who aren't too blind with ambition to see it. The ranks of any field, no matter how mundane or exciting, are full of people who have stretched to get there. People not quite smart enough for medicine still practice medicine. People not quite dedicated enough to law are still lawyers. People who aren't particularly mechanically minded still try to fix cars. This is why a good mechanic stands out, he or she is competing against people who aren't really good enough to be there.

What I am proposing is that we be honest with ourselves and instead of stretching to be the dumbest person at the level above you, choose instead to be the smartest person at the level below you. You're guaranteed to get there and the effort is not large. Over ambition is a ticket to underachievement and in the case of the medical profession, it's downright selfish.

This is why being a software tester was a better choice for me than being a software developer. As a software tester I was competing with people who stretched to get there. These are odds I like. Why would any sane person put themselves in the reverse situation? I'm all in favor of setting goals and reaching them. Climb those mountains, sail those seas, tackle your fears! My point is that there is advantage to be had in ordinary people setting ordinary goals. You're always competing against people you can beat.

One of these days we may live in a world where no one stretches too far; it would be a world where everyone was imminently qualified to do their job. No fakers, no pretenders, no one scratching to get by. Until that happens there is an opening for ordinary people to stand out when doing ordinary things.

114

References and Further Reading

Itching for more? Well fear not, there is a great deal more to be said about creativity in general and how to wield it for maximum career and life impact. If you'd like to read more from the author, several books and many blog posts are available.

Both www.docjamesw.com and www.medium.com/@docjamesw are repositories of James' more recent work. There are also two books on the Amazon kindle store that may be of interest:

Career Superpowers (https://www.amazon.com/dp/B00MEOV48C) is a compilation of career guidance called "super-powers" of which creativity is just one. There are eight others that will help you wield your creativity to maximum impact to further either your personal or career success.

Career Stories (https://www.amazon.com/dp/B017JDMIC8) is an exercise in storytelling about many adventures that have helped formed the author's creative soul.

They are all true and reading them may help you become a seeker of stories as you live your own creative life.

Finally, the following references were used during this book and may be a good starting point for additional research in neuroscience's take on creative processes.

Amabile, T. M. (1996). Creativity in context: Update to "The social psychology of creativity." Boulder, CO: Westview Press.

Anderson, J. V. (1992). Weirder than fiction: the reality and myths of creativity. *Executive (19389779), 6*(4), 40. doi:10.5465/AME.1992.4274468

Baas, M., Koch, S., Nijstad, B. A., & De Dreu, C. W. (2015). Conceiving creativity: The nature and consequences of laypeople's beliefs about the realization of creativity. *Psychology of Aesthetics, Creativity, and the Arts, 9*(3), 340-354. doi:10.1037/a0039420

Beaty, R. E., Benedek, M., Silvia, P. J., & Schacter, D. L. (2016). Opinion: Creative Cognition and Brain Network Dynamics. *Trends in Cognitive Sciences, 20*87-95. doi:10.1016/j.tics.2015.10.004

Cotter, K. N., Pretz, J. E., & Kaufman, J. C. (2016). Applicant extracurricular involvement predicts creativity better than traditional admissions factors. *Psychology of Aesthetics, Creativity, and the Arts, 10*(1), 2-13. doi:10.1037/a0039831

Fink, A., Grabner, R. H., Gebauer, D., Reishofer, G., Koschutnig, K., & Ebner, F. (2010). Enhancing creativity by means of cognitive stimulation: Evidence from an fMRI study. *Neuroimage*, *52*1687-1695. doi:10.1016/j.neuroimage. 2010.05.072

Flora, C. (2016). The golden age of autodidacts. *Psychology Today*, *49*(4), 60-88 9p.

Griskevicius, V., Cialdini, R. B., & Kenrick, D. T. (2006). Peacocks, Picasso, and parental investment: The effects of romantic motives on creativity. Journal of Personality and Social Psychology, 91, 63-76. http://dx.doi.org/10.1037/0022-3514.91.1.63

Hirt, E. R., Devers, E. E., & McCrea, S. M. (2008). I want to be creative: Exploring the role of hedonic contingency theory in the positive mood-cognitive flexibility link. Journal of Personality and Social Psychology, 94, 214-230. http://dx.doi.org/10.1037/0022-3514.94.2.94.2.214

Kandler, C., Riemann, R., Angleitner, A., Spinath, F. M., Borkenau, P., & Penke, L. (2016). The nature of creativity: The roles of genetic factors, personality traits, cognitive abilities, and environmental sources. *Journal of Personality and Social Psychology*, *111*(2), 230-249. doi:10.1037/pspp0000087

Kets de Vries, M. R. (2014). Doing Nothing and Nothing to Do: The Hidden Value of Empty Time and Boredom. *INSEAD Working Papers Collection*, (37), 1-22.

McGuinness, P. (2015). Flow and Mental Performance. *Hang Gliding & Paragliding, 45*(7), 18-23.

Sinclair, K. (2015). The Art of Asking; or, How I Learned To Stop Worrying and Let People Help. *Library Journal, 140*(6), 51.

Sligte, D. J., De Dreu, C. K. W., & Nijstad, B. A. (2011). Power, stability of power, and creativity. Journal of Experimental Social Psychology, 47, 891-897. http://dx.doi.org/10.1016/j.jesp.2011.03.009

TEDTalks : Al Gore, 15 Ways to Avert a Climate Crisis. (2006). New York, N.Y.: Films Media Group.

Wilkinson, A. (2015). The Creator's Code. *Creator's Code*, 1.

Made in the USA
Monee, IL
19 July 2022

99994486R00069